creating a leader

simply
powerful
STAGE TWO

creating a leader

simply
powerful
STAGE TWO

Kelly A. McCormack

Wayland, Massachusetts

Creating a Leader Publishing Division
P. O. Box 5164
Wayland, MA 01778
www.creatingaleader.com

Printed in the United States of America
First Printing, 2018
ISBN 978-1-945943-01-0

The information contained within this book is strictly my opinion from my personal experiences. This book is not intended to be a substitute for the medical advice of a licensed physician. Readers should consult with their doctor in any matters relating to his/her health. If you wish to apply any of the ideas contained in this book, you accept full responsibility for your actions. This includes any support that you may need if you have adverse reactions to reading this material.

The Leadership Score™ and Creating a Leader™ are trademarks of Creating a Leader.

Edited by Leslie Conner and Maureen Schnur
Cover and interior design by Desktop Miracles
Interior formatting using Desktop Miracles design
by Kelly McCormack
Illustrations by Kelly McCormack

dedication and acknowledgement

This book is written for you, the leader who is courageous enough to see that we can create a better world around us.

I acknowledge you for continuing this path into the most powerful, most creative and limitless version of yourself.

I wish you great success as you make your world a better place for all.

Enjoy the journey!

contents

Welcome back, Leaders!

The format of this book will
be similar to the first book.
We will dive deeper into
the work we have started.

And we will look at new concepts critical for any leader who wants to perform at the level that is possible for each of us. The first book was like taxiing on the runway. This second book is about taking off and climbing to cruising altitude. Let's buckle up and have some more fun together!

CHAPTER ONE

the human complex

True leaders are courageous and powerful.

Let's face it…Life IS Messy!

We are born into a world having to operate the most complicated equipment and processes on the planet…ourselves. This is done with *no owner's manual*. This experience could be a recipe for disaster.

Fortunately, we have enough people over many, many millennia who have observed what they could about the *human complex* and shared their thoughts with us. That makes it possible for each of us to come into this world and find experiences and education that advance us past the previous generation, at least most of the time.

Picture buying a new car.

If suddenly our auto dealers' lots were stocked with models from the year 2118, would you want to take a test drive? Imagine what you might see as you sat in this new "car" and turned on the ignition. Um, where's the ignition?!

To put this into perspective -- 100 years ago, we may have been sitting on a train while watching the fortunate Model T owners drive contraptions that seemed "high tech" at that time. These high-tech features included four tires and a steering wheel. A modern-day car company would be out of business if it decided to have so few features. Many of us wouldn't even look at a car that didn't have cup holders!

If no one showed the owner of the 1918 model how to operate the vehicle, he would have to teach himself to drive. Perhaps he would invent new and unintended ways to operate the car. Maintenance could be inadequate. An understanding of the need for oil and tires could be all but lost on him. To go from then to now is a big jump, as we look at the feature-filled cars we have today. Making this more complicated, the growth trend in technology is far faster now than in the past 100 years. We can predict that significant changes will transform transportation over the coming century.

At the auto dealer with this futuristic line of cars, we could take a spin with no training or instruction.

At this moment, you are standing in front of a shiny new 2118 SunPower Radiant transporter. It may not even have wheels. Does that raise the stakes around learning how to operate this on your own? When you sit in the seat, you notice the control panel seems as complicated as a commercial airplane from 2018. As you begin to fumble around to see what will make this vehicle move, you notice that your stress level grows.

With every passing minute, you are more confused, and your frustration level increases. When you do find the right controls that make the transporter move, you bump and knock into everything in your path. You have little control over what you are doing. You are so concerned with your life at this point that you don't even worry about the damage you are doing to the vehicle. Having damaged the vehicle, you purchase it to avoid the expenses of repairing it. Good move!

Note: I do understand that the 2118 model will likely be fully automated, but that would take away a useful analogy. So here, I am describing an increased trend of complications in the operation of the vehicle for purposes of looking at the human complex from another viewpoint.

A week later, you are more comfortable operating the transporter. It seems like you are no longer risking your life each time you take it for a spin. Yet, as we look at the vehicle, there is damage all around it that happened when you were unaware of how to operate it. Thus, your vehicle drives a little off course, and others are not kind to you when you get into their path. This causes you to overcorrect, damaging other parts of the vehicle.

Over time, the way your vehicle operates and your lack of awareness of how it is supposed to operate take a toll. You find one day that the vehicle won't go in the direction you intend. Another day it goes backwards. And finally, it doesn't go anywhere.

Without an owner's manual to provide some education, you lost out on learning about the full capacity of this vehicle. Imagine finding out in the end that you had paid for a vehicle that could have operated at far greater speeds, called flow mode, and taken you to places you hadn't even dreamed were possible. You might feel upset that you had destroyed the vehicle without an opportunity to drive at this higher level. You might wonder why other people were better able to operate the vehicles they bought.

Was there something missing that made this more difficult for you?

the human complex

There are many levels of the human experience that make up the complex that *is* each of us. Understanding these aspects and how they work can make life very smooth. The bumps from early life until the present moment are created because of our misunderstanding of how our complex was designed to work. These bumps change how we go through life. They change our course. They present stops for each of us. They take us out of flow mode, a built-in feature in this human complex we were provided here on earth.

Let's find some perspective on this human complex. Each of us is born into a world that is rotating at speeds up to 1,000 miles per hour, moving around a star at 66,000 miles per hour. This doesn't even consider the rotation of our solar system and our galaxy.

As many as quadrillions or quintillions of animals roam the earth. Yes, that is billions of billions! The innumerable plants that exist, the air we breathe, the water we drink, and the food we eat all represent the complexity of the experience on this planet.

Many of us live in houses that have running water and electricity, both recent additions. Languages are now spoken and written, also relatively recently in the big picture. While information seems more infinite than ever, education is getting more specialized AND broader. Cultural expectations for our social and work roles are increasing.

And technology has changed *everything* in the past few decades.

The human complex has been adapted to many of these conditions, with tremendous improvements over time. Earlier models could withstand the conditions of the planet while getting basic needs met. Later models have adapted so quickly that they can research any topic any time of day within seconds because of advances like the internet. The early models couldn't read, write, or create visions and realize them. The modern model can contact her husband on a free video phone called Skype when she is 12,000 miles away to say a simple "good night!"

The conditions for humans have changed so drastically in a hundred years that our complex has not adapted to all of the changes. These types of changes take time to integrate.

Effects of poor integration can be found in health statistics. In America, as many as 1 in 3 adults have high blood pressure, and only 1 in 3 find themselves at a healthy weight. The body is telling us we are missing some very important details about *how to operate the human complex.*

owner's manual

You are born into this world donning a body which grew from two cells that miraculously found each other, perhaps on a cold winter's night.

Hi, there! I just traveled an impossible journey to find you.

Debra, let's get out of here.

Jane, you are on of the pickiest eggs I know!

Two cells united and intelligently multiplied into tissues and organs that work together to make up a body that you like to call "me."

How does an eye get made?

What intelligence must be present to create a liver that will spend a lifetime detoxifying the stupid things that you put into your body? Really, what on earth is so complex that it grows on its own from two cells? How can those two cells only require a mom drinking and eating enough and providing a home to survive? No, really, I am asking!

We need to add more complexity to the idea that two cells grow into a fully-developed body if we are to begin to see the scope of this human complex we operate.

We all have a mind and intelligence that helps us to navigate in this world. If we have a robot, we must program the instructions that we want the robot to carry out. We would change those instructions when we wanted to change what the robot was doing. The software that represents instructions that we want carried out is programmed and stored in the hardware of the robot's control panel. In this case, we are the robot's intelligence.

When we use our intelligence to determine what we want to create in this world, we are supported by or challenged by what is already programmed in our mind and body.

Here is an example of this. If I want to run a 10K road race, I have several aspects that must come together to make this happen. First, the mind must be on board to make it possible to sign up for the event, train, and then go to the event. Second, my body must be in good enough condition to withstand the race. And my mind can take this opportunity away at any point in this process by telling me it's too hard or by making me forget about it.

Within our minds, we have a conscious part and an unconscious part. Imagine we want to consciously manage the inner working of our bodies every minute of the day. After a few nights of staying awake to keep the heart beating and the lungs breathing, we would be glad to put programs in place that do this for us.

These programs are in the body and mind. This is our hardware and software. Let's imagine a human complex that hasn't been programmed yet. I could say, "I want to run a 10K."

My intelligence could tell me to schedule the event. And I would because nothing is in my programming that tells me not to. I train and get the body strong enough to go the distance. My brain connects the appropriate neurons (brain cells) to make this activity called running more and more automatic. When race day comes, I will likely find my way into a flow-like state, known to athletes as "being in the zone." I created this state because I trained appropriately, was prepared, and was ready to put myself fully into the race and enjoy it. My mind was helpful for navigating this process, not hindering me.

One more layer of complexity will illuminate this process further.

Emotions

Emotions can be wonderful as a part of the human experience, but very little *practical* education is available to navigate them in a healthy way.

They can create destruction in our human complex with an uneducated driver at the wheel!

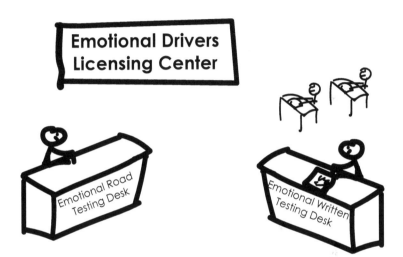

Mom, did you see how I navigated right around anger and into compassion?!

Yes, nice job! And we will practice more on an empathetic response to the girl crying and you can take your test again.

As we will see in the coming chapters, we have an amazing *high-performance human complex*. It can create experiences, changes, connections, and accomplishments. It can even bring the most jaded individual to a state of pure awe. We are driving the most complex machine and processes that *can* exist on earth. We drive an intricate and complicated machine, and *we are not given a formal owner's manual to operate it*.

In some ways, it would be great to have a perfect owner's manual and follow it to the letter. We wouldn't have to deal with earlier dings and bumps in the unit that caused it to operate improperly now. But then, where would the fun be?

None of us was given the equivalent of an owner's manual that worked fully. We are all dinged and bumped in certain ways from our childhood and past. The dings and bumps make it possible to put on unwanted weight, to have increased blood pressure, to lack fulfillment of our desires, or to fail to create something that is important to us.

Two ideas give me a lot of hope.

One, we can *stop producing new dings and bumps* that make it harder for us to create as leaders.

And two, ...

...we *can* reverse our past dings and bumps.

Think of the latter as the equivalent of our guy with the 2118 model transporter doing some major mechanical and body work. Most people had more of an owner's manual in life than he did for his vehicle. Basically, the amount of work involved in becoming a high performance human complex is partially dependent on how complete and true our owner's manual was from our childhood until now.

Owner's manuals are passed down from generation to generation. Way too many innovations occurred in the past century for the owner's manuals to be updated to accommodate the current pace of life. Because of this, most of us got an incomplete and inaccurate owner's manual.

I have experienced many bumps and dings. Thus, I invested more than 12,000 hours to help me understand how to stop creating new dings and how to handle the bumps from my past.

Having done this work, I realize that I am far better off than most of my peers who started with similar owner's manuals. I envision that sharing my learning in this 3-book series could save leaders *a lot* of time and effort.

Most may find their bumps and dings are more easily handled than mine were…and still are. No comparison necessary here. My hope is that I can write this clearly enough that you feel like you can create more limitlessly and powerfully, while saving a huge investment of research time and expenses. As you leap frog ahead to find new ways to update your owners' manuals, I will benefit from your findings and your experiences of life.

In this new and more responsible way of being, we are all better off creating together, in harmony with our human complexes.

Because we are starting
an owner's manual, I have
created a roadmap. This
will help to keep us clear
about where we have been
and where we are going.

You may find that this book
contains more foreign
information than
the first book. Hang in
there. We will get through
the process together. This
book series -- like life -- can
present challenges that, when
overcome, bring us to a new
level of power to create.

First, let's outline
the overview of the
owner's manual.

In this book
we will look at:
Operating Instructions,
Troubleshooting,
and a feature that fosters a
High-Performance
Human Complex!

In the next book, we will
see what the leader uses to
create at higher levels of power.

The
Operating Instructions
are next.

This would be best-case
scenario for operating
the human complex
if you don't have too
much faulty programming.

Even if your programming
wasn't great, these operating
instructions will help you
clean up your human complex
and operate it really well as
you skillfully reprogram it.

CHAPTER TWO

the operating instructions

Operating instructions are critical for any activity that we want to do. If you are like me, you can just make them up as you go after you pull that new machine from the box. Sometimes that requires a phone call to the manufacturer after turning on the right button at the wrong time. But for the most part, machine operation or furniture assembly is usually simple in nature.

Many would never fly by the seat of their pants. They don't know how to put those 67 screws into the Ikea cabinet correctly without the aid of the wordless illustrations provided.

It is one thing to have operating instructions and not use them. It is another realm completely to be without them and to operate something extremely complex based on "hearsay."

I wouldn't want to be at the wheel of the space shuttle without instructions when the countdown begins: 3, 2, 1, BLAST OFF! But even space crafts are simple compared to the human complex. Human complexes *made* them!

Schools, libraries, and the internet are full of instructions that are intended to give each of us a better or more productive life. But does having a library in my community mean that I have an owner's manual to run this human complex that I call "Kelly?" Apparently not.

Maybe there is something to distilling the information in a simple and practical format. Maybe it is necessary to use a different language to understand things we have heard all of our lives, which may be critical to our well-being. Maybe I needed to go through enough challenges personally and professionally to enable me to bring this information to you with lightness and humor. Whatever the reason, ...

...let's start a good owner's manual now.

In many cases in this book, I have chosen new language. As discussed in the first book, words can carry baggage. Much of how the human complex works is misunderstood because of our reactions to certain words. Some of our reactions reduce our power to create because they take us off the path of the most effective version of ourselves.

Our limiting beliefs can reduce our ability to perceive our best options.

When a word doesn't match our programming's definition, it creates problems. If we are trying to increase our power to create, moving past our limiting beliefs and opening ourselves to unfamiliar ideas is part of the process.

For simplicity, let's look at the human complex in three parts. Talking about parts is helpful *only* to get a sense of the concept. In reality, the parts constantly interact and affect each other. For example, if we upgrade a limiting belief that afflicted the mind, this can improve the body. When we think about something scary, our bodies react to these thoughts. No *part* of our complex is "more important" than the other. They are ALL critical to operate appropriately.

This concept is like an astronaut wearing a space suit for a spacewalk. The two become one complex. The astronaut provides intelligence and movement. The suit provides a safe environment and a constant supply of life's basics, like oxygen and warmth.

I have faith that new language and ideas combined with commitment to move past old habits will create an even more fulfilling life for each of us.

I will do my best to support your journey with concepts that I have learned through my research and experiences. It is up to you to take what you see as helpful, navigating responsibly through your own circumstances in life. Everyone is different, yet we can all fulfill our potential if we understand the mechanics of it.

intelligence

The first part of the human complex is *intelligence*. It was challenging to find a word for this critical area that is a hotbed for differences in opinions, beliefs, backgrounds, and viewpoints.

But I've seldom shied away from a challenge, so let's just jump right in…

Intelligence, for purposes of defining this level of the human complex, is everything that is beyond the body, the emotions, and the autopilot functions of the mind. *It is our creative power source.* It is our creativity. It is the potential of who we are before we program the body, emotions, and autopilot functions of the mind. It is something greater than our "*selves.*" It is the clarity of the vision we hold when we know that it has purpose. It is the captain who changes our course in life. It is the source that fosters a beautiful piece of art. It is the birthplace of transformation. It is the well-spring of flow mode. And it feels darn good!

Intelligence can be called the source of flow, a higher purpose, the creative plane or realm, our best selves, or peak performance. It is who we are being when we are self-actualized, as Maslow calls it. I call this the source of +10 leadership, which amounts to fulfilling our highest potential through access to this power to create. This is what made us what we are, literally, from two cells.

There is nothing to fix or do with this level of our existence. Nothing can go wrong with a source of power and creativity, in and of itself.

We *know* when we have connected to our own power.

In that state, we flow – peacefully, joyfully, courageously, and powerfully – creating improvement for ourselves and those around us.

Think of Intelligence as a power supply. It's like plugging into something greater than yourself.

If you have ever felt like something was effortless, you may have had the feeling of Intelligence in action. When we connect to this source, life just *flows*!

The creative power supply of intelligence *can* be reduced or cut off by malfunctioning parts of the human complex. Let's begin to unfold how the parts beyond intelligence are supposed to operate when the human complex is in a state of fulfilling its potential.

emotional/mental

To keep the simple, three-area approach to the human complex, we will cover the emotional and mental aspects together.

Each of us has a *bucket*. That bucket is filled with a recording of every detail -- the 5 senses, thoughts, feelings, emotions, bodily sensations, and beliefs -- of every moment from before we were born until now. Additionally, the recordings that were made when we were unable to process them fully – because they were just too good or too much to handle – get an extra helping of vibrancy to stand out.

Stuck in between those recordings or pictures are the meanings or beliefs that we gave to our life's circumstances and ourselves. They act like a pair of glasses. These beliefs change the way we see the world. Unknown or misunderstood, these beliefs can detour excellent leaders into survival mode, sadly only observing their unfulfilled potential.

We covered the 3 areas of unconsciousness in the first book. Let's dive deeper into each of these areas to take better control of our emotional and mental processes. They are a great springboard to clear a path to the flow of our creative power.

education

Education is a combination of all the recordings we have in our buckets. We know that when we are missing education, both learning and experiences, we are less capable of interacting with life. Just like our guy who was test driving his 2118 SunPower Radiant, ...

...we tend to get banged up a bit in life when we don't know what we are doing.

Meanwhile, education is an excellent tool for us to learn how to take the reins of our lives. It helps to put the most intelligent part of ourselves firmly and comfortably into the driver's seat. Imagine knowing enough about how the entirety of "you" operates so that you could steer it like the captain of a ship and take it to whatever destination that you choose. The captain doesn't have to constantly turn the wheel. He is simply setting the direction and correcting course as necessary.

Our education and experience levels need to be closely matched to our challenges. Too large of a gap between the two can make us frustrated and unfulfilled. We have options to program a smooth path to our highest fulfillment mode called flow. For this we need to understand how to use the features of our human complex.

Activity: Make a list of the struggles you find in the different areas of your life. Create an action for each that would begin to resolve those challenges.

We can begin to look for educational deficits in our personal and professional roles. For example, maybe I notice that my public speaking is not up to the level that I need it to be. Perhaps my teenaged son is isolating himself more than what seems healthy. Or I notice that I become anxious every time I use a spreadsheet. My list of actions may include some public speaking training at Toastmasters, a conversation with a mental health professional, and an online Excel course. Recognizing struggles that stem from missing knowledge and training can reduce the chance of creating other types of adverse unconscious bugs.

beliefs

Each of us has a special programming unit that acts like an *autopilot function* in our human complex. This is a feature of us that *can* behave more like a machine or a robot, and it is comprised of two components. First, we have the *experience recorder* known as our education. And second, we have a *focus mechanism* that is known as beliefs.

A belief *is* a limiter.

When we assign a meaning to something, we reduce the additional possibilities in our minds. We would never think about using a fork to comb our hair, because that is *not* our belief about forks.

Honey, thank you for getting me a dinner fork for my hair. It is *sooo* much faster than the salad fork was.

Beliefs are useful when we want to find ways to describe, assess, and tell stories about our experiences. Otherwise, we might walk around like little children looking at everything in life in awe without naming anything or deciding what the object of our attention means. While there *is* a definite place for that child-like view of life, beliefs do affect us – positively and negatively – as we shall see.

Meanwhile, we need to understand that we are wielding a very powerful tool when we create or adjust our current belief system – a belief system that is shaping *and* limiting how we see the world and ourselves.

A great use of a belief would be to support the operations of our human complex.

"I am worthy to participate fully in this world."

Beliefs are damaging when we adopt something negative about ourselves or the world.

If these happen frequently or in a critical moment, the belief gets recorded in our programming. This limits the operations of our complex.

"I am not good at math."

It's payday!! Here is your money.

That's okay, Boss. You keep it. I'm not good at math.

These limits imposed on our lives can come in many forms of beliefs. In general, a belief is something that we experience as true that changes our perception. That does not mean that the belief *is* true, but our programming says it is.

Someone could believe that the sky is dark during the day and blue at night and have it fully programmed in their nervous system. Since they live on this planet, we know this specific belief is not true per the definitions we have assigned to day and night. This one is obvious. Most beliefs have more of a hint of truth to them when they are limiting us.

A couple of unconsciously programmed beliefs are common among us. These beliefs come in a form that sounds something like "I am not safe" and "I am not worthy."

Beliefs shape our perception organs and processors.

Our beliefs focus our attention and bring into our experience the contents of their programming. This becomes our experience of life. Therefore, it seems critical for us to find those limiting beliefs and adjust them when appropriate. Let's look at different types of beliefs. This will support us in spotting them more easily AND help us stop programming new ones that block our power to create.

Hard-coded beliefs can be categorized in two ways. One includes everything as a child we programmed from our caregivers. The second includes our interpretations of the overwhelming – traumatic and peak – experiences that occurred in life. Because of the slow brainwave levels during our childhood, caregivers' beliefs are often stored as our own.

Additionally, the human complex records our overwhelming experiences for quick recall, like favorites on an internet browser. What we decided about ourselves or the world in those moments are programmed directly into the unconscious mind. In both circumstances, we are hard coded with beliefs, many of which are disempowering. These hard-coded beliefs strongly shape the actions and behaviors of our human complex.

Rules and expectations are beliefs that become "the way things have to be" for us to feel comfortable. They are so unconscious to most of us that we can easily miss that this is *only* the way things are *to us*, based on our programming. Some of these expectations and rules are important to our well-being and need to be upheld. Some of them are leftovers from earlier times in life and don't support us any longer. We can spot them in statements like, "I couldn't believe that she did something like THAT!" To find your rules, ask yourself "What must happen for me to feel good about this event, person, job, haircut, success, etc.?" If you find that *a lot* must happen for you to feel good, it is time to look at your rules. Life flows more easily when we release unnecessary rules and expectations.

Meanings and stories are the narrations we create for our experiences that change our viewpoint in life. Events and objects lack meaning until we assign it to them. A neighbor is just a neighbor, until we assign her the meaning of "friendly" or "nosy." Stories create a narrative that can make us believe something about a person or an event, whether true or not. When someone takes the last paper towel, leaving an empty roll, I can make it *mean* they are inconsiderate. I can tell a *story* about how this always happens to me, or I can grab another roll.

We don't think of these as a choice because meanings and stories are so ingrained in our daily experience of life. We become the product of the meanings we assign and the stories we tell. Better to tell stories that support our complex!

Decisions are like high-powered stories and meanings. When a real decision is made, it cuts off all the other possibilities that you didn't select, and it narrows your focus. That is the function of the belief system mechanism – to narrow the focus.

Decisions are a tool. They are neither good nor bad in themselves. They are damaging when we use them to lessen empathy for sections of the population who look or live differently from us. Decisions can be helpful when we realize that the one pair of jeans in our hand fits great, and the other twenty don't work for us. *That* decision makes our husbands happier because we can now go to the checkout counter.

Intentions, goals, and visions are like decisions in that we are creating and focusing on a possibility that we may make into a reality. Again, these are neither good nor bad by themselves, but the power they hold makes it important for us to watch the content we decide to put into them.

A vision of our daughter going to a great school can be a motivator. However, a vision of us failing in a certain area of life *can* hold our attention long enough to turn this belief into a reality.

These are tools, sharp ones. Wield them with great care.

Values are our deeply programmed emotional priority makers. If I value adventure over security, I will likely have a life that is different from someone who values security over adventure. These *can* be changed with some deeper work. We can get somewhat familiar with our own values by looking around at our house, car, and other purchases and decisions. We will begin to see trends. The automakers know this and craft their slogans to make sure they reach us. Read the one from the maker of your car. It may reveal something interesting.

Identity and roles are last in this list, but they are of great importance. They affect us daily. These tools are so profound and effective that their use can immediately change everything about who you think you are. The words "I am…" should come with a warning label.

Warning!!

Anything combined with the words "I am…" CAN be hazardous to your health. Proceed with Caution.

As soon as we adopt someone else's negative opinion of us (for example, "I am *stupid*"), our brain and mind go to work on reducing our capacity to perceive and process the environment around us. In that way, we make what they are saying become true for us.

These are not hard-coded beliefs, but they are fast at programming the nervous system and the subconscious mind. This makes the conscious use of the words "I am…" a very effective change agent for an instant upgrade to our human complex. Replace a repetitive "I am not sure…" with "I am on this!" and mean it. See what happens. But we must *mean* it as much as we mean the unkind things that are said in our weaker moments…and maybe replace those too. Anything that follows the words "I am…" needs to support who we want to be.

It creates identity!

Understanding these various types of beliefs may make it easier to see what *language patterns* we have been using. That helps to assess our current perspective, which hints at our Power to Create on the Leadership Score. Most of us can find some beliefs to improve. If we invest in understanding and altering our beliefs, we improve our lives and the lives of those around us.

I have referred to a belief as a pair of glasses that warps our view of the world. We *can* adopt broader beliefs, such as "We are all in this thing called life together." A shift like this could enable us to see the challenges and messiness of life, making us less likely to judge unimportant differences between us. Possibilities begin to magically appear in all areas of our lives when we take off the limiting glasses and put on clearer ones.

To find beliefs that were programmed in our lives, we can look at all the places in our current circumstances in which we are struggling. If we have handled our educational deficits but still find great challenges, then we are likely to have at least one of these types of beliefs limiting us. Finding them is like seeing a pair of invisible shackles that we can now take off.

This increases our power to create as effective leaders.

Let's do a quick recap:
We are looking at the
operating instructions
for the human complex.
The first layer of the human
complex is intelligence.
This is experienced as the
feeling of something
"bigger than ourselves"
and it supplies our
power to create.
Then we looked at our
mental and emotional levels
of the human complex.
This is the part that usually
keeps folks unplugged
from their power source.

Much of the programming on mental and emotional levels could be represented by a bucket. It could also be called the autopilot function. The bucket "contains" our recordings from the womb until now -- known as our education -- plus our beliefs that limit our focus in the world. The third and final part of our bucket is next. We will look at the special way that the nervous system records overwhelming situations -- known as traumas.
Go with courage!

traumas

So far, we have looked at the contents of our bucket, which includes our experiences in life that provide us our education. Additionally, the bucket includes the beliefs we assigned to ourselves and the world around us. The third and final area of our bucket is the special mechanism in the mind and nervous system that highlights the recordings of overwhelming experiences within our complex. These are known as *traumas*. This is a stigmatized word in our society, but learning about traumas is key to making the human complex perform at its highest levels. What we don't know about traumas is most likely keeping us unfulfilled!

We can all handle a certain amount of emotional impact during any experience we have in life. This is called our *resilience level*. Everyone's is different.

Humans have evolved to record the situations that are beyond our resilience level in an unconscious storage location that shields us from the full emotional impact. This is a safety mechanism that helps us to avoid similar experiences in the future OR to finish processing the circumstance when we are safe.

The details of the recorded trauma are stored in something akin to an *emotional doggie bag*. The unprocessed details in the doggie bag can be "digested" later, from a more resourceful place.

If we didn't learn that this doggie bag *feature* came with the human complex, we would have to keep nearly every doggie bag that we ever brought home! Buying a new refrigerator might seem like a better option than opening the one filled with all the doggie bags. But no worries. We all have these doggie bags. It may be time to "open the fridge" to see what doggie bags might be there -- unprocessed and running your life in adverse ways – and we will look at specific methods to do that in the Troubleshooting chapter. With practice, handling the contents of our doggie bags is like taking a shower or brushing our teeth.

Emotional traumas are *injuries* to our nervous system...

...caused by experiences in which we were scared, embarrassed, hurt, or diminished in some way that *threatened the quality of our lives*. If we were *unable to defend* ourselves or *leave* the circumstance, and we felt *isolated* and unsupported in that moment, our nervous system created a freeze point. That freeze point in the nervous system opened a new *doggie bag* that recorded all the details of what was happening around us *and* within us.

An analogy for this freeze, or injury to the nervous system, would be to imagine if a bullet got lodged into a muscle.

Ouch!!

If that happened, we may need to remove the bullet to support the function of the body. If we don't remove it, the body will change the way it functions to compensate for this bullet. The "owner" of the bullet may experience pain from trying to function normally in life. The compensations for this pain may cause him to be less active. If he got the bullet taken out, he might find that his pain level would be gone, his compensations could be worked out of the body, and his activity level could go way up -- maybe back to where it was or even better.

Our experiences in life, the meanings attached to those experiences, and the past traumas lodged in our nervous system can lower our resilience. Our resilience can be reduced enough to make us feel threatened *more* often, unable to defend ourselves or leave, and to feel isolated in many of our life's circumstances.

Low resilience can make life's events hit us like an *emotional bullet* to the nervous system, leaving us unable to process the situation in that moment. That "bullet" makes our hormones and neurotransmitters react to provide as much safety as possible during the perceived threat, which changes the way we perceive *and* record the details of that moment. The bullet, or emotional impact, punches a hole in the subconscious mind, initiating the new emotional doggie bag.

That emotional bullet is lodged in the nervous system, causing us to function differently until we release it. If the bullet stays in place, we will still be subject to the reactions of the negative sensory recording in the doggie bag. That means we are subject to a fight-or-flight response to *anything* that resembles the details of the recording. That includes any sights, smells, tastes, sounds, tactile and internal feelings, thoughts, emotions, bodily sensations, and YES...

...the beliefs that are hard coded and do run our lives.

If an emergency room doctor had a patient come in with a bullet wound, that doctor would not massage around the wound instead of removing the bullet. That would make no sense, and the patient would suffer from such illogical care.

Because our society is not familiar enough with emotional trauma bullets, most of us are doing a lot of massaging around our emotional bullet wounds. A better *solution* is to remove the bullet (release the freeze in the nervous system) and process the contents of the doggie bag (resolve the recording).

Before I understood traumas, I was looking for more ways to massage my own bullet wounds and avoid the effects of the unprocessed doggie bags in my life. My compensations made my life smaller and far tougher to live, making it harder to reach my potential. Even the "massages" -- the glass of wine, calling a friend, a shopping spree, or building a business -- suddenly weren't the "fix" they used to be. The effects of traumas wreak a bit of havoc on our lives.

Because we all have traumas, it is wise to get them handled as soon as possible. If we manage them, we are less likely to pick up new compensations, limiting beliefs, or traumas, providing greater access to supportive experiences in life.

Increasing our power to create involves resolving our traumas and limiting beliefs.

There are benefits to traumas in the human complex. They are programmed to make us avoid perceived threats to our survival. Because of the trauma mechanism, we humans are still here!

But, as we have seen, there are downsides to this mechanism if we don't process the bullets and baggies that are holding us back. Those downsides get worse over time.

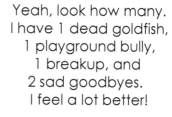

Look at all the bullets you took out! What's in the doggie bags?

Yeah, look how many. I have 1 dead goldfish, 1 playground bully, 1 breakup, and 2 sad goodbyes. I feel a lot better!

Warning!!

*Not acknowledging
and processing our
"bullets and baggies"
has been known to cause
relationship weirdness,
chronic illnesses,
unfulfilled potential,
and other symptoms.*

If we fail to process the bullets and doggie bags in our nervous system and unconscious mind, we could experience some pitfalls. One of those pitfalls is *projecting*. This is a big problem for the greatest majority of us, due to a lack of understanding how our beliefs and traumas work in the nervous system and unconscious mind. They are affecting us moment-by-moment, without our knowing it. The unconsciously recorded relevant and irrelevant details of traumas can retrigger the trauma experience in our body and mind whenever our environment resembles *any part* of the recorded details. We think our reaction is based on our current circumstance, but it is being processed through an earlier trauma.

Oops!

As an example, let's say a blonde coworker at a past job betrayed my confidence. My unconscious response could be to avoid all blonde women in the future, especially when I am being asked about my personal life. The trauma is keeping me "safe" by taking the current environment's details and comparing them indiscriminately with the past recording. When I encounter a new blonde woman at work who asks me something even mildly personal, I react with the trauma's emotions and sensations -- like betrayal, mistrust, and anger. The non-related blonde now sees me as unable to communicate well and a bit *twitchy*. The problem with my inappropriate reaction is that **this** blonde is my new boss.

It's time to handle the trauma!

Another pitfall from traumas involves the beliefs programmed during those moments that are still controlling us. Imagine I was unprepared for a meeting presentation and received criticism from my boss and colleagues. Unable to comfortably receive the feedback, it hit me like an emotional bullet to my nervous system and started a new doggie bag. Stored in the doggie bag was my decision in that traumatic moment: "I shouldn't be in management." Over time, that decision could change my career direction, and I wouldn't be conscious of the reason. The nervous system hard-codes the recording of these beliefs when a trauma occurs, like our early childhood recordings.

If we only had one or two traumas in life and they were in very different circumstances from what we experience daily, we would likely have no issue. But each of us has dozens to hundreds of traumas that are recorded. Because we don't know that they are retriggered, we are recording new experiences that include the old trauma content. This can make for a bad pattern. We can change this pattern.

Traumas *do* steal our power to create by blocking us from our intelligence and creative power supply. And they wreak havoc in our attempts to operate this human complex in a fulfilling manner.

When we know how to resolve traumas and limiting beliefs, we handle them – like maintaining a car.

No big deal!

We have covered the 3 areas of unconsciousness that make up the bucket that each of us possesses. This amounts to our autopilot system plus the bumps and dings that make our human complex go off course. Yet, we live in a world where we are not alone. Therefore, we need some operating instructions to include interactions with others.

We have seen how each of us has a bucket and that bucket is *plugged into our creative power source* -- our "Intelligence."

healthy interdependence model

If we have a bucket, then others must have a bucket as well. In the Troubleshooting chapter, we will cover the challenges that can happen when the buckets get together, especially cracked ones and those with lots of unresolved doggie bags. For now, let's look at a *healthy interdependence model.*

Healthy Interdependence Model

John   **Jessica**

"Intelligence"   "Intelligence"
Creative Power Supply   Creative Power Supply

In this example, we have two buckets interacting. John and Jessica are both dinged up a bit, and each has their own programmed limiting beliefs that make them less capable of interacting with the world around them. But they are still able to stand on their own without having to depend on someone else to take care of their bucket and without having to take care of someone else's bucket.

When we look at less empowered examples in the Troubleshooting chapter, we will see that this example would be a rather healthy one in our society. With relatively healthy buckets, each takes and gives in ways that support both. They are *both* better off for having interacted. Communications are forthcoming and boundaries are in place. Both are quite comfortable that they will be okay in life and are balanced and comfortable with others having opinions and differences.

Healthy relationships are more obvious when compared to challenging or less empowered ones.

This brings us to boundaries…

What are boundaries, anyway?

Imagine if you had the chance to clear out the *bullets and doggie bags* that affect you, if you could consciously see and adjust your *beliefs* to support you, and if you attained the *education* necessary to comfortably interact with your environment.

Further, imagine assessing which purchases and accomplishments from your past were influenced by insufficient programming. Seeing that, you change the decisions that no longer support you. For example, you sell the house that you purchased to show your father you *could* be a success and you buy a more affordable house.

If you did this until you eliminated the sources of stress in your life, you could enjoy well-being without the need for anyone else to do, be, or say anything.

At that point and from that place, **what crap would you never put up with from someone else?**

You just found your boundaries!

They are your bucket. They are the edge of your comfort zone. If the edge *is* kept in place in an empowering way, and you've handled any threats to your survival that would result from maintaining those edges, then you have healthy boundaries. This **skill** requires us to know how we feel.

Healthy boundaries are essential to fulfilling our potential.

The bucket represents our *autopilot programming system*, plus our dings and bumps. In addition, we have a *control panel*.

So, the bucket is our autopilot programming, our comfort zone. It has our recordings and our beliefs. And some of the recordings were made when we were overwhelmed. The missing education, the beliefs that need to be reprogrammed, and the traumas that need to be released and re-recorded are the bumps and dings that cut our power off.

The next tool is
going to be the control panel.
Think of it as a bunch of dials
that represent our character.
We can have character-building
courage or patience or empathy.
Our contol panel shows those
character muscles that we have
built for ourselves. It also ties
back into the bucket and the levels
of the human complex based on
our knowledge, emotional well-being,
and our power to create.
If we don't handle our bucket, survival
mode will take over our control panel
and will rob us of our power to create.

control panel

Each of us has a panel of controllers that are part of our human complex. Imagine you have a courage dial. That dial moves from low to high and is affected by your programming in life. Some find their courage is high when they are at home, singing and dancing with the family. That dial may move to low when out with colleagues at a karaoke bar. Our programming has created defaults on our courage dial that move to certain levels for certain experiences.

But what if we could move that dial for ourselves? What if courage could be generated, and we could step onto that karaoke stage and belt out our best version of New York, New York -- Frank or Liza style? What if the dial could be set on high as we watch ourselves cross the room to meet the interesting person who caught our eye? What if we put the dial on max and decided we could create what we want, taking one courageous step at a time?

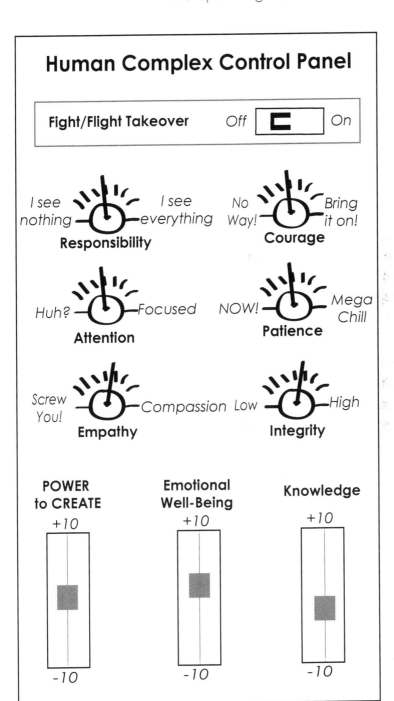

"Stuck dials" challenge the functioning of our human complex. We can intelligently operate the complex to the level that we understand the controls. When we are missing education about the function of these controllers, we operate based on old programming.

Let's look at how some of the dials may be holding us back. With this understanding, we can learn to move ourselves forward. *Courage gives us the ability to act despite fear. Responsibility allows us to perceive what is happening.*

If we turn up the courage dial, we will see the responsibility dial was set on low. We can turn up the responsibility dial to recognize where we are in life and how we got there. Low responsibility reduces our understanding and hinders our ability to create.

Quickly raising the dials from low to high has consequences as well.

Most of us would be somewhat traumatized if we turned up the responsibility dial and saw how we have been hurting ourselves and others in various ways.

The more we turn up the dials without a subsequent increase in our emotional well-being, knowledge, empathy, and kindness, the lower our ability to process what we have been doing on *autopilot mode*.

I just turned up my responsibility dial and realized that yesterday I interrupted someone in a conversation.

But, Frank, you've been doing that for 20 years!

As we learn to increase our knowledge and emotional well-being, all the other dials become more adjustable. When we find greater levels of peace within ourselves, we can create enough internal safety to increase many of the other dials. I recommend that each of us make our own list of dials so we know what tools we already have. These dials *and* the programming we have in our human complex are major points of leverage for each of us to live a more fulfilling life.

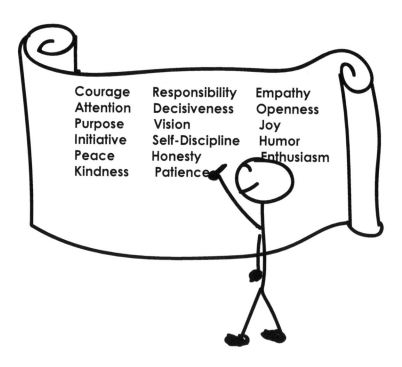

Courage	Responsibility	Empathy
Attention	Decisiveness	Openness
Purpose	Vision	Joy
Initiative	Self-Discipline	Humor
Peace	Honesty	Enthusiasm
Kindness	Patience	

super powers

We may not have capes, but the more someone has been through and resolved, usually the more strength that person has within them. Imagine you are holding up an extra 200 pounds of weight! If you resolve the issue that created that "weight," all you are left with is the strength that came from holding it up. You can now use that strength in a different way. The compensations and strengths that make us hold up, move around, strategize through, or grow more resourceful in life's challenges become amazing *super powers* when the original traumas and limiting beliefs are resolved.

Is that a new cape that you are wearing, Resourceful?

Yes, thanks for noticing, Vig!

Huh? What?!? Did somebody say something?

physical

The third part of our human complex is the physical body. This is the obvious, visible part of us, and usually gets the most attention. In the human complex, the physical body could be thought of as similar to the space suit in the earlier drawing. If the space suit is like the body, the astronaut represents the other two levels. These are exhibited through the autopilot and intelligent modes. The astronaut is the driver.

This becomes important when we are working to create as leaders -- using the body as one of our greatest resources and troubleshooting it when it isn't operating well.

Let's take an example. Matt, a thin 10-year-old, was approached one day by his best friend, Paul. Paul told Matt that he was too skinny and would never be strong enough to do anything. Other boys overheard this, which embarrassed Matt. And Matt valued Paul's friendship, so this was a painful experience. This created a bullet and a doggie bag in Matt's human complex. After that, Matt was never able to maintain a healthy weight, despite workouts and high-calorie meals. When Matt was 28, he spoke with a friend's mother about his weight. She shared with him that there may be something that could help with this. She then helped Matt to "remove" the bullet and "digest" the contents of the doggie bag.

Four weeks went by, and Matt called his friend to let him know that, for the first time in his life, he had put on 10 healthy pounds with little effort.

The body responds to our intelligence and our programming. There is visible evidence of this. When a person gets out of a toxic relationship, they look 10 years younger.

Most of us were brought up to look at the body as the place where the health issues originate. In most cases, there is a lot to be found *beyond* the body when we want to resolve issues *with* the body.

If the space suit is going in the wrong direction on a space-walk, we must go to the astronaut to change that. Telling the space suit to change direction would be frustrating, at best.

This is NASA.
We are checking in with
the spacesuit to see how
you are doing before your
next spacewalk. Over.

What the...!?!

Though the body may be responding to our conscious and programmed commands, our body *is* still a critical component of our experience in life and needs appropriate fuel and maintenance to operate well. Without that, the body can adversely affect our experience of life. Improper maintenance could worsen the programming of our autopilot function and our access to intelligent and flow modes, which are discussed further in the next section.

Since this is an area in which most are familiar, let's look at a few *basics of operations* for the physical body.

Our *nutrition from food* needs to be as clean as possible to help the body to process it efficiently. If we include processed foods in our diet, the nutrition content is lower and the elimination process is more taxing. We all have a good idea of what foods make our bodies operate cleanly and efficiently. With a little adjustment to some beliefs and adding a bit of creative power, we can turn the healthy and energizing foods into a fun, enjoyable, and artistic experience.

Our *hydration* is critical to the processes of the body. Our bodies are an electrical, chemical, and mechanical masterpiece. Sufficient hydration helps these processes to work as they are designed.

Our *air and breathing* contribute to our power to create. Air is what we consume every second of our lives. Breathing fully, as the body was designed, gives the body its proper resources to make us energy machines.

How we *move our bodies* and how much we move our bodies makes a big difference in how well our autopilot and intelligent modes can work. Each of us has an appropriate type of exercise and movement that allows the body to perform at its best.

Our nervous system -- the brain, spinal cord, and nerves – are housed in our bony structures, like the skull and backbone. If our *posture or structure* is not aligned as it is designed, that misalignment can create wear and tear and hamper communications throughout the body and the mind. This reduces access to both intelligent and flow modes.

Helping the body to *clear or cleanse* the excess stress, foods, chemicals, pollution, and other toxic inputs can keep the body in its best condition.

Getting appropriate amounts of quality *sleep* can help the body generate new cells, clear out the unhealthy ones, and process the day's events so they don't start to "stack up in our mind."

I recommend that we become students of what works best *for us*.

Everyone has unique bodies and has had different experiences in life. Each of us must determine our formula for how we operate our body, and this can change over time. When we feel low, we may reach for poor-fuel foods. When we improve our complex, we may begin to crave the foods that make us feel great.

That completes the levels of the human complex. We looked at the level of intelligence, which is our power to create. The level of mental and emotional includes our bucket and control panel. And the physical level of our human complex supports or diminishes our access to our power. Now that we understand the 3 levels or parts of the human complex, let's look at the 3 modes in which we can operate.

3 modes of operation

The human complex can be operated in 3 different modes. These are known as autopilot, intelligent, and flow modes. Let's look at what each of these modes does for us.

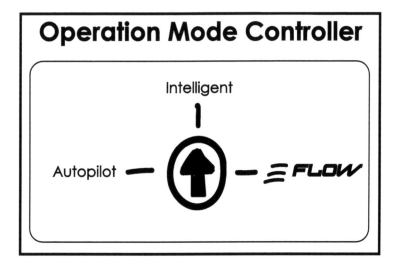

Autopilot mode is just what it sounds like. We rely on the current programming in our bucket, set the dials on the control panel, and let the "habits" take us through our days. This can be a great mode for handling more creativity in our lives. Autopilot mode fails when we don't realize that relying on our programming from when we were 5 years old is not always the most effective way to create what we want in our lives.

Intelligent mode is the one in which we are creating something new. Basically, this *is* leadership mode for envisioning what we are going to create.

This is the captain's position of setting the course and steering the human complex to the desired destination.

One feature of Intelligent mode is to "check in" on autopilot operations to see if everything is programmed appropriately to get us to where we are trying to go. If we are looking to build a business or teach our kids, we need to know what that would look like in the form of a vision or goal. We would also want to handle the programming needs, like education and supportive beliefs, to get there. Intelligent mode does this for us.

We can stay in this creative mode of intelligence more often, opening new creative abilities that aren't available to us when we are in autopilot mode. This mode can even upgrade the connections in our brains' neurons as we do new, exciting, surprising, or engaging activities.

If we learn to use the autopilot and intelligent operating modes more and with greater skill, the final mode becomes a possible option for us.

Flow mode is just that. We flow. It is a combination of autopilot mode and intelligent mode. But it is magnified to the point that it seems like the human complex falls away, and the activity is like a wave we are riding. There is no self-consciousness, only genius or the feeling that we are a part of something bigger than ourselves, especially when this mode is at a peak. It is the most efficient, effective, and feel-good mode that we can find. This mode has been sought after for millennia and is called by many names in different cultures and circles. We will look at flow mode in greater depth in Chapter 4 as we explore the high-performance human complex.

society

As we have seen when we looked at the healthy interdependence model, we are not alone. Therefore, operating instructions should at least highlight that society has an impact on each of us, and we have an impact on society.

Our own body, mind/emotions, and intelligence are comprised of numerous systems that are working together to make the most out of our intelligent orders and autopilot programs.

Society is similar. We are all small units of a bigger complex. That complex needs intelligence in the form of conscious direction, creation, and improvement. It needs to have programming in place that works to the benefit of all who are a part of it. And it needs to have a physical structure that supports it. With practice, we can begin to recognize these in any society of which we become a part.

Let's integrate what we have learned with a short story and then look at the Troubleshooting chapter of the owner's manual. To get to high performance, we may need to do a little "body and mechanical work" on our human complex. Investing in this now can mean years of increased power to create more of what you want to experience, see, and do in this world.

What do you think of the show?

Interesting so far. I wonder where it will go after the intermission.

the
central story

"The Play of Life"

As an author, I sat down and decided very clearly on the goal of reviewing the book you are reading now for my own final edits. At some point, I notice *I am playing music and preparing food instead.* I am clear that these activities are NOT the same as editing my book. I have just been consciously introduced to my first cast member in the internal play of my life. Each of us has various "characters" who exist because of some of the challenges we have experienced in life. This cast member is inattentive and capricious with flavors of stubbornness and self-centeredness. She doesn't want to stick to a schedule. She wants to do what she wants to do when she wants to do it. I am going to name this character "Windy." There are more cast members and all of them are there, whether I acknowledge them as how I feel – or not.

Unacknowledged, they run my life through a very chaotic form of autopilot mode. They aren't necessarily keen on intelligent mode – what I want -- as that undermines what *they* want. Life is an impromptu play with characters who are known and visible in our lives, like friends and family. Additionally, there are these "characters" who are running our internal play of life. These "characters" are running my life and the lives of others. These internal players help determine our overall, well, *character.*

I engage Windy. Realizing that I want to edit this book while she is interested in anything but editing, I ask what she wants to do. She wants to play, learn, walk, sit in the sun, go on vacation, create a new business, and become an excellent speaker...ALL in this very moment! I smile. She doesn't understand why she can't do everything *right now.* After a conversation about what that would look like and how we could do these things over time if we engage in discipline, she relents in a "wait and see" posture. But at least she does relent. The music goes off, and the food goes into the refrigerator to be prepared at meal time.

Time to sit down to edit. I start by opening the document containing this book. I begin to read the copyright page when another character appears. He is out of breath and clearly overwhelmed. He wants me to know that this is way too difficult and that I am not skilled enough to write and publish this book. There are too many unknowns. It might be a failure, and it might be a success. It is going to be a lot of work, and the work I do might be wrong. The people who get this might judge me and the...

"Stop right there!"

I am calling this one "Melvin."

"Melvin, what are you looking for?"

Melvin is confused about what he might be looking for. He simply knows that none of this will work out. After some conversation, Melvin reveals that when I take a risk on doing something new, I might be judged, or fail and judge myself. He is trying to protect me from getting hurt. I assure him that we can find new ways to handle the consequences when life goes in a different direction than expected, *even* when I take risks. I share with him the plan to finish the book and engage the editor *and* the consultant, both of whom would ensure that the message was clear, concise, and accessible. They wouldn't steer me wrong, and others would be there to support my efforts with experienced and professional opinions. He, like Windy, is reticent, but relents. He accepts that I'm going to take this risk. Since he is aware of the plan, he allows me to complete my task.

With that, I finish reading the copyright page when Windy shares she is done with this discipline thing. After all, it had already been five minutes!!! I share the outcomes once again with Windy and reiterate the plan with Melvin. Now I move into the Table of Contents. The next character shows up when I review the bullet points representing Chapter 3. He is insistent that the Chapter is not perfect. He goes on to say that nobody would understand a chapter about trouble-shooting and that I had not done a good enough job with it. I will call this character "Perry." He and I talk about having to do this *perfectly* and how that has kept me from finishing the book for weeks. We come to an agreement that my very best in a specific timeframe would be good enough and that Perry could start meditating and doing yoga when he felt like my best wasn't good enough for *his* standards.

Taking inventory, I realized that a great deal of my life had been run by Windy's capriciousness, Melvin's insecurity, and Perry's perfectionism. And I was only on the Table of Contents! How in the hell have I run my life at all with these characters fighting for the starring role? It dawned on me that the intelligent mode -- that is available to each of us who are ready to move past chronically stuck autopilot mode -- requires that we become the star of our own internal play in life. These internal characters can support our goals when we listen to and help them. To do that, we must see them for what they are: a re-activated feeling connected to unre-solved traumas from when we were younger, unsupported, and overwhelmed.

I am curious about who will show up next in my internal play of life. Onward I read. *Chapter 1, The Human Complex.*

After acknowledging the increasing internal tension, I am clear about what is boiling up from a simple title. "Melvin, I WILL explain what that means to my reader. Perry, I will explain it to the best of my ability! And Windy, you DON'T get to turn on the internet until 1 hour from now!" I have a very strange daycare-like situation going on here, and I have only met three of the participants. Surely there are more. I look at the first illustration in this book and...

...APPARENTLY, Windy takes over the starring role as I just found myself checking a new email on my phone. I have been given an opportunity to deliver a speech on Wednesday evening. It is Monday morning as I write this. Melvin just took a Xanax. Windy thinks this is the greatest thing ever, and we should write 10 speeches and pick the best one. With Windy's suggestion and the short period available, Perry gets into a yoga pose and proclaims, "Ohm Ohm," drowning out the obvious violations to his standards. Despite this cacophony, I do have to decide if I will write and practice a speech in the next two days. But for now, back to Chapter 1...

I look at the first illustration in this book and assess whether it will be clear enough to initiate curiosity in the reader. I have turned down the volume from the first 3 characters, who are all giving me unsolicited advice. And I am finding a new character emerging. She thinks she's an artist and is an opinionated one at that. She has a lot to say about the illustrations in my book, especially my stick figures. My stick figures were born of a desire to communicate somewhat heavy concepts in a light and playful manner. I fully recognize how far short they fall from Perry's standards of Picasso, Monet, and even my friend's 4-year-old daughter. But they are a form of communication. This new, emerging character seems to be a cousin to Perry -- in her opinion around the standard of quality that I have chosen -- and a sister to Windy – in her demands for the amount that she would like to see happen *right now*! Her main concern is having the fullest creative expression that can come of this book. She shows up complete with a beret, a brush, and a paint pallet. She represents my creative side and I will call her "Marie-Pierre."

Marie-Pierre's first concern is that I haven't detailed or shaded the illustrations to her liking. She is also feeling the loss of an opportunity to put links in the eBook that will allow the reader to look at related videos -- *that* change she would like to see me make right now. She then moves onto a conversation about t-shirts, mugs, and training programs when I interject. "I can't do all of that at once!" This startled Marie-Pierre. After all, she knows that I consider myself to be a creative type, and I have a desire to serve. Why wouldn't I want to do everything possible creatively to help the reader to get what they want to learn? I explain to Marie-Pierre that all of this is a learning curve for me. Each function -- from writing to illustrating to video creating -- takes my hard work at not only learning what to do, but also getting around the entire set of internal characters that make up the play within me. When I go back and forth on new projects, it freaks out the various characters in different ways. Although a part of me wants to do everything at once (and I am not naming names – Windy), the clearer part of me recognizes that it's not possible. I will have started many projects that will come to a point of frustration in the learning process with little sense of completion. That won't be good for anyone. I may even create new characters who hold me back if I choose that strategy.

Another strategy could be that "we" get this book written and published as well as I can produce it right now. There is leeway to make updates to this book or write new books in the future. I can blog after the book is written to add new and different concepts. Videos can be made, to support the needs of my audience. All of this can roll out, but it will start with a book that is as good as I can make it right now, with "artwork" that is as clear as I can create right now. Marie-Pierre looks at me and asks if we could put a few extra details on the illustrations. That is just fine with me.

With that, Marie-Pierre takes on the role of Creative Director in this impromptu play of life. She understands the need for space for me to finalize the book, so we can move onto the other creative projects. She knows that the players would need to be aligned for their strengths, while handling their concerns. She gives Windy the job of Chief Learning Officer, beginning with everything she could learn about publishing. She gives Melvin the job of Chief Health and Mood Officer, ensuring that I am eating, sleeping, and exercising enough to bring me into flow mode. She turns to Perry to be, of course, the Chief Quality Officer. But his new standard considers my current skill level, the amount of time available, and the desired outcome, and NOT world-class performers! Marie-Pierre handles the concerns of the others as they come up, and everyone feels comfortable with this arrangement. She even requests that I hold off on doing the speech until I could finish writing this book. I happily agree. With that, I find flow mode and go from page 1 to the end of Chapter 4, supported by my "crew."

Perhaps the impromptu play of life is easier to star in when I realize I am not the only actor in this play. Becoming the director of my own play could be as simple as acknowledging the feelings that these players have been sharing. From there, I can help them resolve the overwhelming situations from which they came to exist. Meanwhile, I can make sure that they are acknowledged and know what production is running right now.

I found out about
Internal Family Systems
after writing this central story.
Learning more about that
work became a rapid path to
improve my power to create.
That tool and others, which I will
introduce in the next chapter,
are the basics of how the
human complex works. I look at
all of these tools as studying for
a license to successfully drive
the human complex.

CHAPTER THREE

the troubleshooting section

We are traveling on a planet that races around a star at mind-boggling speeds. We are driving a human complex that has an autopilot function that most of us don't know we have. We lack practical and consistent operating instructions from birth. What could *possibly* go wrong in *that* scenario?!

Nuclear Plant Control Room

the leadership score

Navigating in this world can be complicated no matter where we start our journey in life. We already have dings and bumps that make life a bit more challenging. The great news is that most of these issues can be handled in ways that bring the body and mechanics of our human complex back to intended operations. We can even advance to flow mode!

The road map that helps us to bring our human complex back to a great condition is the framework that was introduced in the first book. The Leadership Score™ is a model that helps us to assess our *Power to Create* on a scale from -10 to +10. This scale can help us to debug the areas in which we are losing our power to create.

The scale starts at a *fully competitive and comparative state* called -10 leadership, in which we are engaging in a zero-sum game that doesn't support us or others. The most empowered version of ourselves would lie at +10 leadership, which is akin to finding our flow mode. 0 is neutral. In this neutral state, we find ourselves neither strengthening nor diminishing ourselves and those in our environment. Those below 0 have a courage and responsibility dial that is set too low for them to see clearly what is happening in life.

Many of us spend most of our time in this range called survival mode.

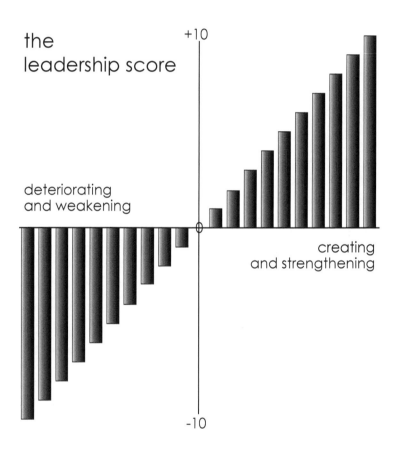

the
leadership score

+10

deteriorating
and weakening

0

creating
and strengthening

-10

the leadership score

power to CREATE	visioning	executing	empowering	developing
+10 creating	all possibilities visible	effortless	inspiring	continuous
0 neutral	neutral	neutral	neutral	neutral
-10 competing	all obstacles visible	limited	discouraging	non-existent

This book is designed to help each of us understand the human complex and begin to straighten out what isn't operating well. Once we have accomplished that, we can express the competencies found in The Leadership Score: *visioning, executing, empowering,* and *developing.*

To support us in using these leadership skills to create, this section of our owner's manual will help us *troubleshoot* some dings and bumps that make it more challenging to operate our human complex.

Global Human Complex Troubleshooters' Anonymous Meeting

This section is designed just like a troubleshooting section in a manual for a machine. Five groups of challenges will be presented, starting with *Clearly Defining Leadership*. If a challenge or a group doesn't seem to apply, please feel free to skip it or skim quickly. Many say they learned something from each section that could help with other people when it didn't apply directly to them. This section will likely be the heaviest lifting in this book. I will touch base at the section's end.

clearly
defining leadership

Let's dive into the areas introduced in the operating instructions and troubleshoot our Leadership Score to increase our power to create.

Challenges...

I don't consider myself a leader, or I don't think of leadership as the Power to Create.

Life is becoming a competitive rat race. I am constantly trying to get my basic needs met. It seems there must be more to life than this.

Potential Steps...

Try on the identity of a leader who has Power to Create. You have enough Power to Create to read to this point in the book.

Find ways to increase your power.

Take a walk -- clear stress, encourage the relaxation response, and improve access to your power supply.

Find a limiting belief and improve it. For example, if uncomfortable when talking with the boss, ask yourself what might you believe to feel that way? If you feel unsafe, give yourself proof that you are safe, or do something about your life to make that true.

If you are incompetent in an area of your work, learn what is necessary to become fully competent.

Find and complete an improvement project.

Clean one cluttered drawer that you have ignored.

Help your child overcome one school challenge.

Envision a really small improvement in your life and put it in place (finance, relationship, work, etc.).

Have an honest conversation with someone.

Challenge...
I don't feel like I am creating to my potential.

Potential Steps...

Our creative power supply is always available if we trouble-shoot the other areas of the human complex that get banged up and stop this flow.

In the third book, visioning and executing exercises will help free you to do the steps to creating. This *can* back you into handling the human complex impediments.

If you know there is an impediment and you can't find the problem on your own, find an experienced person to help you. This could be a coach, a therapist, or an **honest** friend.

Challenge...

The more I read, the more overwhelmed I get. My life needs a major overhaul!

Should we "test" it or do we just "reset."

This one is going to require a "reset!"

Potential Steps...

You are in good company. I recommend baby steps and giving yourself a celebration with each one you take. An infant's smaller attempts to walk are encouraged and celebrated until he is *transformed* into a toddler. Take each of your steps, accumulating them until they *transform your life.* Do something special for yourself, like making a meal that you know you love.

Start 1 or 2 daily habits that you think you might do after resetting.

Walks, self-care, learning about healing, nutritious eating.

Find one support person to help you.

Challenge...

The information you are sharing doesn't feel right to me.

Potential Steps...

I am sharing my experience. Don't let that present any threat to your experience of life. It is a great idea to *listen* to yourself without *projecting* onto me.

Ask yourself:

> *Am I ready to improve some aspect of my life?*
> *Am I willing to be uncomfortable in the process?*
> *Will I do what it takes to make the change?*
> *Will I take full responsibility for my actions?*

As the captain of your own ship, you need to take control of what *and* when you learn.

The Buffet of Life

What did you select
from the buffet?

I selected what I was
willing *and* able to digest.

Challenge...

I don't feel like I want to create more in my life.

Potential Steps...

If you are already fulfilling your creative potential, expanding where you can in life, and society is benefiting from your empowering contributions, then you would likely not feel this way. A healthy human experience often makes us want to continue to learn and expand. +10 leadership is akin to a first black belt. We are competent creators who empower. Then we have fun creating even more!

Troubleshoot the 3 areas of unconsciousness and "stuck dials" on the control panel.

When I start a project, do I feel fear that makes me want to quit? Get a trauma expert to help you.

Do I feel fear doing a specific responsibility at work or home that I haven't been taught? Learn it!

What if my courage has gone down instead of up as I am getting older. Do something that you feel would require courage. Get a book and take yourself to lunch or dinner. Practice and do a speech for a crowd whom you know will appreciate it. Sign up for and run a 5K. Celebrate your accomplishment.

Review the mechanics of creating in Book 3.

Be very kind, gentle, and patient with yourself.
This is work!

Bear in mind that a **ship** is changing course!
Exercise self-compassion, Captain.

Challenge...

I don't know what competition looks like when it is hurting us.

Potential Steps...

If we compete by challenging ourselves and others in a healthy way that supports all involved, that is a great use of competition. But it is rare. In our society, we are living the definition of competition based on power-stealing comparison.

Picture this scenario: I am living my life and happily enjoying my 2 kids, in my 3-bedroom house, married to my loving husband, and glad to go to work daily. Each month, I enjoy watching the growth of the kids, the successes of my husband, and the creative endeavors that are so fulfilling in my life. I can continue to do this, expanding the health and power of my human complex and what I create in the world around me.

Enter comparison. Suddenly, my neighbor with a 4-bedroom house tells us how he was promoted and bought a car that only those who have "made it" in life can drive.

Find and change the places where you have adopted others' comparisons, including those of society, to your detriment.

Do I feel worse about myself with certain people, shows, commercials, or magazines?

If I had nothing to lose, what would I want in life?

Where can I release my comparisons and be happier?

Challenge...

Help! I am comparing myself and I can't stop!!

Potential Steps...

If I am unaware of the components of my human complex, I can get programmed to believe that others are behaving at a standard that I must adopt. Advertisements may reinforce this. I start judging my husband to be an underachiever. I judge myself as a poor mother. I begin disliking my job. What happened? Comparison happened. It can lure us away from the most powerful versions of ourselves, in which we create at our best levels.

If steeped in competition, at negative levels of the leadership score, increase your power to create toward your version of a +10 leader.

Practice valuing yourself for being you, with no regard for accomplishments. We're all just big kids who could use some extra love and caring!

What is in your life that makes you grateful?

If no one was watching and you couldn't see what others were doing, what would you want for yourself?

Power to create will make you comfortable enough to never *compare* with someone else.

Find every place where you are reduced by your comparisons and get clear about what YOU want instead.

Power increases when we run our own race.

mastering the bucket

Challenge...

My resilience level is getting lower as I am getting older.

Potential Steps...

This can become a common occurrence in our 30s, 40s, or 50s. Imagine what it would be like to see what limiting beliefs and traumas are doing to us in a visible form. If the "invisible" were depicted by a person, he might become more bound by ropes that represent his beliefs, finding movement more and more difficult. He could have heavy loads stacked on him from his traumas. But because these ropes aren't visible, they can seem unreal. They become visible when you train the "eye" to see them.

Create a relaxing self-care routine.

Epsom salts baths, saunas, meditation, plenty of sleep, nutritious food, gentle exercise, connection with friends or support members, trauma expert, etc.

Get professional support to resolve the traumas and beliefs that are reducing the recovery of the nervous system.

We will look at EFT with Matrix Reimprinting.

Work with a coach or therapist to set up a life that fosters resilience.

Challenge...

My bucket seems to be missing a lot of education.

Potential Steps...

The driver's seat in the human complex requires enough education or "experience recorder" to take on new challenges.

Use a gap analysis for your creative endeavors. For example, if you are trying to become healthier, look at the details of your vision and your current state.

Clarify as much information as possible about the vision and the current state.

Solve your challenge, or gap, skillfully.

Become a student of the area for which you seek competence. In this example, study various nutrition programs, cleansing, and exercise to attain physical health.

Bonus

Josh Kaufman has a TEDx talk and a book titled *The First 20 Hours*. Invest 20 minutes into his talk or a few hours into his book on **rapid skill acquisition**. You can save thousands of hours while supporting yourself to competently fulfill your potential.

Josh Kaufman
TEDxCSU

Challenge...

I have a belief that it is difficult to learn.

Potential Steps...

Because beliefs are ideas that we have adopted and supported by our reasoning, we can start knocking out the supports for the belief. The example of a belief like "it is difficult to learn" can be changed.

Challenge this belief by remembering several times when it *was* easy for you to learn.

Set up a reasonable challenge that proves you can learn easily when you set it up well.

Learn to sew a button, learn to do a single yoga pose, follow one simple recipe to create a meal, find one feature in the car's owner's manual which you didn't know was there, or draw pictures.

The more that we challenge and knock out any support for the old belief, the more our nervous system and mind begin to adopt new beliefs like...

"I can learn anything when I set it up well."

Hey, Fred, what are you doing with the key?

I just used it to unlock the invisible shackle of another limiting belief.

Challenge...

I am not conscious of my meanings and stories.

Potential Steps...

Look at the world around you for a moment.

Understand there is *no* meaning assigned to it. For example, if you are drinking a coffee, the mug that contains the coffee is just a mug. If we want to say the mug is "good" -- a meaning -- that has nothing to do with the mug. We could easily say that the mug is bad. Still doesn't make a difference to the mug, the world, or anyone else. That meaning only affects you. You affect others if you are unconscious of these meanings.

Recognize that we are constantly assigning these meanings and making stories about how things are in the world. But they *aren't* that way in the world. They are ONLY that way in our programming.

Think of a situation that is uncomfortable for you. Ask yourself what meaning you gave to the situation.

An example: My boss is being less communicative with me. I ask and decide it means I am not doing my job well. (Turns out he had a personal problem. Oops!)

We tend to like to hang around with people who have similar programming, making it look like our stories and meanings are truer than they are.

Have coffee with someone from a different background. Appreciate their stories of life.

Challenge...
The world is a scary place to be for me.

Potential Steps...

Stories are fantastic ways to communicate a message to symbolically teach the nervous system and the mind. And meanings *can* be very moving emotionally. Both are tools. On the one hand, stories can show how the human complex can be challenged and become stronger -- great lesson. On the other hand, they can tell us that the world is scary, unsafe, competitive, or that we aren't enough. Obviously, this is not a great use since these beliefs change our programming.

Find a positive meaning in the experiences of life.
At least I shared a deep friendship before she moved.
Although I was laid off, I learned a lot from my job.
Resolving traumas made me more self-compassionate.

Adopt beliefs in the form of stories and meanings that will shape the way you want to see the world. Choose your stories!

Realize you are projecting your meaning on the world, but you are the one who gets to keep the meaning you created.

We may chuckle about the curmudgeon down the street, but you can *imagine how many unconscious meanings and stories that person told about the world around him to arrive at that state.*

Challenge...

I have "high standards," but I feel like that may be hurting me and others around me.

Potential Steps...

While rules and expectations can represent standards -- or perhaps more accurately, boundaries -- they aren't always good. Life is never quite so cut and dry. The edge of our comfort zone is represented by everything that is still programmed in our nervous system, including disappointments in early childhood.

Inspect your rules and expectations.

Find where you are disappointed. See if you have a rule or expectation that is supportive -- or not.

Do you expect someone to come over who said they had to work?

Your expectation would breach their boundary.

Ask someone else or do something else!

Advanced

If "external changes" in life seem like they will make you happier, you will find internal work to be done.

Your new boyfriend left when you asked him to change his hair color, job, and name?!!!

I know! It's as if he doesn't understand "high standards."

Challenge...

I want to handle my traumas and associated beliefs.

Potential Steps...

The nervous system is always trying to work through the unresolved traumas. When we behave more resourcefully in a new circumstance that resembles the traumatic scene in some way, we may be able to resolve some of the old impact to the nervous system. Take a deep breath and let the old stored emotions find their way out of the system without trying to change it with a drink or a movie. It is attempting to finish "digesting" the emotions that got stuck during the trauma. This is a method of "chipping away" at the old traumas.

Do EFT with Matrix Reimprinting with a practitioner. This can be a complete method to handle both the bullets and the baggies – including beliefs -- associated with traumas.

Read *Transform Your Beliefs, Transform Your Life* to educate yourself about traumas.

Look at the CDC-Kaiser study about Adverse Childhood Experiences (ACEs). This can be a motivator to do the work.

Find a therapist who is a trauma expert. Educate yourself on trauma so you can find a qualified one – this *can be* rare. There are solutions. But you must look for them.

Spend more time creating, which makes use of intelligent mode. That can be healing.

Challenge...

I have had overwhelmingly positive experiences that I have been trying to reproduce for years.

Potential Steps...

Overwhelmingly positive experiences can create the same situation in our mind and nervous system that traumas create. Anytime we are overwhelmed within a positive or negative circumstance, a recording starts in the subconscious mind. In that case, our programming didn't support us to be present enough to observe the situation and let it pass, just like any other situation would. This "positive" -- but unconscious recording -- is running in the background searching for situations that can approximate the peak moment again.

This can set us up for repetitive or addictive behaviors to fulfill an unconscious need to experience this peak again.

This can often be found and resolved with EFT and Matrix Reimprinting work.

Work on increasing intelligent mode while overcoming any areas of stuck autopilot mode.

Do you have a belief that says daily life is mundane without that peak experience?

Perhaps, create a belief that you "enjoy the little things in life" and act on that belief by smiling at a flower, a child's giggle, or even a red light!

controlling the panel

Challenge...

I see where the dials on my control panel may be stuck.

Potential Steps...

If *courage* is down, then we often can't take *responsibility*. If we can't take responsibility, we can't see what we are doing to create an adverse situation.

Dial up courage step-by-step.
Think of 5 small steps that would take courage.
A phone call, a project, an action, an apology, etc.
Select one that is relatively safe and do it. Repeat.

Exercise courage. It is a muscle.

Find and change beliefs that cause fear-produced reductions in courage and responsibility.
I can't do that. I don't know.

Face fears, then increase responsibility until you find *what you are doing*, as opposed to what others are doing. For example, instead of blaming a boss who is discouraging me in my work, I would focus on resolving my shortcoming, confronting my boss, or finding a new job. I look at what I need to do to resolve the situation.

Handle traumas.

Challenge...

I turned up my courage and responsibility dials, and I need something more to be able to work well with others.

Potential Steps...

Courage increases our ability to face fear while responsibility increases our willingness and ability to see what is happening in a situation. With empathy, we can feel what someone else is feeling. It is a built-in mechanism that keeps us connected to others to avoid hurting them.

Improve your empathy: Darlene Lancer's eBook, 10 Steps to Self-Esteem is a great tool.

Notice where you have turned down your empathy dial regarding any individual or group. Low empathy can block an understanding of others' experience of life, leading to competing in the form of gossip, comparison, prejudice, discouragement, etc.

Look for places where your empathy dial is programmed by society to exclude others:
It's a dog eat dog world out there.
Thank goodness I am not starving, in poverty, addicted.

Recognize beliefs which strip your power to create with others. *He doesn't do that as well as I do. I don't think I fit in. I don't like the way she does that.*

If you have deep empathy issues, traumas are the cause and they need to be resolved.

Challenge...

I feel generally "out of control" on my control panel.

Potential Steps...

Although it can sometimes feel like progress is slow, each change improves all levels of the human complex. At different points in my process, I have looked back and been surprised and amazed by how much progress had occurred.

Focus on using the courage and responsibility that you create to help you with cleaning up your bucket.

The control panel and bucket work together.

Example: Decide you will work on this by finding a small belief that you change to a more supportive one. Then use the courage found from that to do something at home or work that you have been putting off. Use that to propel you to find support.

Challenge...

I would like to do this work faster.

Potential Steps...

Dials on the advanced section on our control panel help to navigate life in a far more skillful manner. Some examples of these dials include forgiveness, gratitude, acceptance, compassion, and love.

Cultivate *forgiveness* to resolve stuck places from the past when you decided others, or you, could have done better. We now know that they, and you, couldn't have done better because of our programming. Forgiveness is a dial that helps us to release the places in ourselves that are stuck in blaming mode. Forgiveness is not about condoning the behavior. It is about releasing our hold on the blame that is cutting off our power.

Find an example of where you are still holding blame for yourself or someone else. With what you read in Chapter 2, look at the situation in a new light and see if it softens enough for you to let it go.

Adopt more empowering general beliefs that support resilience in a variety of experiences, behaviors, and people. **We're all doing our best.**

Be grateful whenever possible. Practice this. It will reduce stress, increasing your power.

We can recover *a lot* of our power from working with these advanced states.

Challenge...

I feel like shame and guilt keep holding me back.

Potential Steps...

Various factors drive the emotions of shame and guilt, cutting off the source of creative power. In early childhood, we may have adopted shame or guilt because of our situation, for which we weren't responsible. This one is handled best with support.

Recognize that each of these destructive emotions may be misinterpretations of your responsibility level for past experiences. With active guilt, you may be taking responsibility for your actions during a past event based on what you would do now. You couldn't have done that then. Programming made you do what you did. Similarly, with shame, you identified yourself -- not just your behavior -- as wrong. The devastating nature of identifying yourself with past events when you were less skilled than now, is a direct path to -10 leadership.

Think of a very small current circumstance for which you feel guilt or shame.

With your new learning, look at the situation. Do you still have a negative feeling? If so, see if you can remedy it. If you were not at fault but still feel bad, a trauma practitioner can help.

Guilt and shame cut the power supply. With this, we feel we must operate competitively in the world.

When we are programmed better...we do better.

3 groups down...only 2 to go.

Clearly Defining Leadership ✔
Mastering the Bucket ✔
Controlling the Panel ✔
Powering through the Modes
Becoming a PowerBuilder

Great Job!
See you soon.

powering through the modes

Challenge...

I don't quite understand autopilot and intelligent modes.

Potential Steps...

Autopilot mode is when we are only engaged in our programmed habits. This is always running. Intelligent mode is when we can move past some part of our programming and make a new decision, action, behavior, or direction in life. It is a big deal to come to the place where intelligent mode can be exercised. This feature separates us from other animals. It allows us to envision new possibilities and execute them. I can be plodding along in my life, doing what my earlier programming dictates, and one day I notice something in a new way and act on it. I continue to do that until my new path no longer resembles my programming.

Use intelligent mode to help you do a task, like brushing your teeth, with the opposite hand. Do this for a week to see if it gets easier. This is intelligent mode bringing you into a new habit – changing autopilot mode.

Change a more meaningful habit that you currently have into an improved one for at least 40 days. Notice when it gets easier as intelligent mode upgrades your autopilot mode.

Challenge...

I want to move out of the stuck autopilot mode.

Potential Steps...

We have 3 modes of operating. On the Leadership Score, these would line up something like this:

-10 to -1	Stuck autopilot mode or survival mode
0 to 5	Autopilot and some intelligent mode
6 to 9	Autopilot run by intelligent mode
+10	Flow mode

Work on the 3 areas of your bucket that you see could use attention.

Ask yourself this question about your human complex, *"Who is driving this machine?"* If it is society, media, family, or the boss, then it is time to take back the reins.

Do it as the driver and not as a passenger in your own life.

Clarify how you feel and act from there.

Get clear on what you envision for your life.

Be more conscious about doing what you are doing right now...and right now...and right now.

Consciously make decisions from intelligent mode more often. This disrupts stuck autopilot mode.

Challenge...

I'm a poster child for the Unhealthy Interdependence Model.

Potential Steps...

Buckets *can* stay intact when we have an upbringing without serious traumatic events *or* negative beliefs that reduce our ability to experience the world comfortably. When this is not the case, our bucket can get cracked, and our creative power supply can leak. There *are* people with bucket issues who will show up to take whatever power has leaked, which can cause further issues with our cracked buckets.

Are you doing what you want to do in your life for your own reasons? Sometimes childhood or adulthood situations can program us to avoid our own needs. Understanding this can help you find a pathway back to self-esteem and healthy boundaries. It is a pathway that is certainly worthwhile.

How can you improve your self-esteem?

Practice treating yourself as valuable by feeling what you need and satisfying that. Make your favorite meal. Take a music lesson that you have wanted to take. Listen to yourself and do something about what you want from a deep place.

If you can't hear what you want deep down, practice self-care to relax daily until you can hear better.

For further support, read Darlene Lancer's eBook, *10 Steps to Self-Esteem.*

Unhealthy Interdependence Model

Mark

"Intelligence"
Creative Power Supply

Christina

"Intelligence"
Creative Power Supply

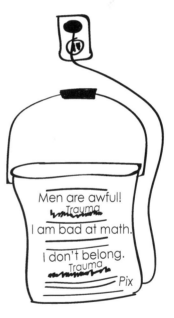

Challenge...

I am constantly defending my bucket. If I am honest, my bucket doesn't even feel like "me."

Potential Steps...

When a child finds it too unsafe to do what their gut tells them to do, they may create a fake bucket. This type of trauma occurs because of the absence of a healthy environment and attachment with our caregivers. This is unconscious and they don't know they have created this bucket. Additionally, highly traumatic events can make this phenomenon occur. The person is operating from a fake bucket that is not plugged into any power source. They are literally starving for juice in life. They are more than willing to take the power that leaks from others' cracked buckets. And unconsciously they are even willing to take over those buckets when they can. This can be called Dominator behavior.

Do you feel the need to control others and see no problem with that? Get support

Do you feel like others who are "weaker" than you deserve what they get? Get support

Find your Dominator behaviors and do some work on them. The effort will restore your power versus taking others' *leftovers*. Start reading different titles from Darlene Lancer. Learn what you can so you can get out of the trap.

Life is better and you deserve it.

Fake Bucket

Challenge...

I feel like I am losing myself in life.

Potential Steps...

Buckets can be overtaken. This usually occurs in childhood. This person is unconscious about what is going on. They just know that life seems hard, and they want to get the people that are weighing them down to straighten up. Because of what has been programmed, they have poor boundaries (cracked buckets). This is Surrenderer behavior.

Recognize that Surrenderers and Dominators are like two puzzle pieces that seem to fit together, but nobody is fulfilled.

Codependency for Dummies is a very practical book to educate yourself. This will help you see that it is NOT about changing anyone else's behavior. It is about learning how you feel about something and moving forward on that to take excellent care of yourself.

Work on self-esteem. What do you want? How can you give yourself the care that you look for outside of yourself? That is self-esteem work, and it may have been missing in your original programming.

Take responsibility to live a fulfilled life.
  Simply commit to this and take each step that comes.

When you do this work, your "puzzle piece" changes shape, and Dominators don't notice you.

Challenge...

I can see how I might have both traits, Dominator and Surrenderer.

Potential Steps...

Let's face it -- traumas suck, and it would be great if we could eradicate them and stop the pattern of passing them down through generations. Dominator behavior is usually done to those who exhibit Surrenderer behavior. It becomes like an unconscious and ineffective 3-legged race for both. Because the Dominator type no longer has access to their real bucket and power, they can't create well on their own. They must find those who are vulnerable enough to overtake, or they feel they will not survive in life. They have identity stealing traumas that are projected on everyone else. Their fake bucket identity makes them unable to have empathy. Either behavior means a lack of checking in with the real feelings you have and acting on those. Healing this takes courage and is best done with trauma-based therapeutic support.

Find "blameless" education on these subjects. (Darlene Lancer's books to start).

If you are trying to become your best self, but feel fearful, unsafe, or unworthy, do trauma work for your own sake.

You may be missing important programming and your flow mode. Do the work.

You're worth it!!

Challenge...

I had a good upbringing, but there are some people at work who are like this.

Potential Steps...

Both types of behavior -- Dominator and Surrenderer types -- are on a *hyper-autopilot mode* that has an extra layer of unconsciousness that makes them unable to see the unconsciousness. This is coupled with poor boundaries. These can cause problems for people who are around them. There are deep responsibility issues, keeping them blind to the negative effects that they are creating.

When you see someone, who is moving too quickly with few boundaries, put in your boundaries – know how you feel and say what is acceptable to you. If they cross your boundaries consistently, let them go – whatever that means for your situation.

Keep in mind, a Dominator will do or say something that would be completely unacceptable to someone with good boundaries. They hand you a *shit sandwich* to see what you do with it. If you take the *poo panini* and don't put in boundaries, they see that they can take your Power to Create from you. Know your boundaries and keep them in place. Set up your life so you are not dependent on someone who doesn't respect your boundaries *and* wish YOU well.

Challenge...

It seems that all of us are susceptible to the effects of Dominator and Surrenderer behaviors. We would be wise to do what we can to understand this well.

Potential Steps...

The more you clear your bucket, the less susceptible you will be to these Dominator behaviors. Remember, those who are fully identified with Dominator behaviors have no access to their power source and are -10 Leaders. They simply have no real power to create. They must compete to get the power they need. Their lives depend on it. It is not a small thing if you are being manipulated by a person with Dominator traits. But with a good understanding of the human complex, you can guard your vulnerability that makes it possible for them to steal your Power.

Surrenderers are usually confused by the Dominators in their lives. They are trying to be helpful, without recognizing that this "help" is a projection -- and not helpful. It is an attempt to have some control in a life that feels out-of-control.

You can come to a place where neither affects you.

Keep working on the steps to ascend the Leadership Score.
  What beliefs do you have that don't support you?

Educate yourself on these two bucket issues:
Codependency and Narcissism – Darlene Lancer

They said on the news last night that rose-colored glasses, like the ones **you** wear, *can* cause cancer.

"THANKS," Aunt Betsy!

Challenge...

I have noticed some areas in my life where my boundaries are weaker or my bucket leaks a little.

Potential Steps...

Most of us who have Surrenderer behaviors didn't get the memo when we were kids that Dominator behaviors existed. There were probably Dominator and Surrenderer behaviors happening around us that we learned to model. Those who were told to walk away from Dominators as children didn't always know why they were walking away. This exposed them to new circumstances their parents didn't warn them about in which they could be manipulated by a Dominator.

Put in boundaries.
> *How do you feel about what is happening to you?*
> *Tell the other person what is and isn't acceptable.*
> *Change your circumstance when they don't listen.*
This patches the holes in the bucket and helps to remove "unwelcome residents."

Once we have handled our boundaries, we can get others out of our bucket. This happens *when we know what we want* and realize it is not the poo panini being offered.
> *Their "poo paninis" can be mean comments, flattery, moving into a relationship too fast, asking for too much information, certain gift giving/expenditures.*

Take gentle baby steps, learn what *you* want, and show self-worth through great self-care.

Challenge...

It sounds like all of us have something to learn from this.

Potential Steps...

We all have some bangs and dings that cause insecurity that is projected into the world around us. If the insecurity is combined with beliefs that make us want to never repeat a situation, we may exhibit Dominator traits. When we are feeling overtaken, cornered, frozen, and without a good choice in a situation, we can show signs of Surrenderer behavior.

This isn't about adopting new or stigmatized labels. This is about what part of our bucket (missing education, limiting beliefs, or traumas) or our control panel makes us think that we must dominate or be dominated. That's it. *If we aren't purely creating, we are projecting insecurity.*

And we need to do our work.

If each of us handles our own...

Challenge...

It feels more bleak hearing about all of this.

Potential Steps...

Learning about some of the factors that have kept us and others stuck on autopilot mode can be jarring at first. Depending on the health of our bucket, it can even create anger to see these things.

Recognize that Dominator behavior types are not conscious enough to know that they are stuck in a manipulative pattern. They are programmed that way, learning to hide their identity or adopt an unreal one reinforced on them.

Recognize that Surrenderers were overtaken early in life, as part of their programming. Nobody is suffering or causing others to suffer on purpose. They are programmed that way, stuck in *that* prison. We should all strive to intelligently operate our human complex to a state of health. And help others to learn when appropriate.

Recognize that all the generations before us are as blameless as we are. We are certainly responsible for our behavior, as were they. Yet, the programming was unconscious.

You can change that now.

Creating a healthier bucket puts all of this into perspective.

Challenge...

As a Surrenderer, I feel like I am behind in many areas. I want to catch up in the areas that are a problem for me.

Potential Steps...

This is a common challenge for those who were brought up as Surrenderers. The great news is that you can very rapidly begin to recognize the qualities that make up these behaviors in your autopilot function *and* the behaviors of Dominators. Once you have done that and are beginning to take small steps toward living *your* life on *your* terms, you can follow what this book series suggests. When you do, you can become super-fast at learning, spotting beliefs, and resolving traumas. With effort and commitment – probably less than it takes to manage the Surrenderer challenges – you will begin to execute the autopilot function in a more fulfilling manner. It does take work, but it really is worth every effort when the results start to happen.

Find resources to learn about codependence – the pitfalls and the path to healing.

Know that every person has experienced neglect of one form or another in their childhood. If the upbringing was good enough – there **may be** fewer problems in the bucket. I loved reading *Running on Empty* by Dr. Jonice Webb. It illuminated places where my programming fell short and helped me to reprogram the autopilot.

Challenge...

I still don't feel like I can readily achieve intelligent mode.

Potential Steps...

Intelligent mode helps to change our programs, expand our experiences, and improve our beliefs. It is responsible for increases in our creative power.

Become inspired by a vision, dream, or goal. If selected well and acted upon, you can fulfill it through finding intelligent mode.

Play a game where you label what is in front of you for one minute. As you consciously decide that *this is a chair and that is a table*, you engage intelligent mode and come out of autopilot mode.

Every time you become aware in this very moment about what you sense -- through your 5 senses, what you feel, think, or believe -- you have found intelligent mode. Practice this! This form of "smelling the roses" is one of many pathways to access creative power through intelligent mode.

(I couldn't draw a rose!)

Challenge...

I want to access flow mode.

Potential Steps...

There are different ways to move through this process. I will highlight a couple of them here.

Method 1

Assess your current score and plod along to become a more "empowered citizen" in your own life. That could mean some work that improves your score from 0 to 1 by simply reading a book series like this and applying some of the learning. Each subsequent improvement could help to raise your score.

Method 2

This requires commitment. Decide that *you are a +10 leader* and then find all the places in which that is not true and change them. Adopting a new identity can highlight the areas that are inconsistent. Chapter 4 will cover +10 leadership in greater depth.

Both methods require gap analysis.

Envision an improvement, assess the current state, and select the steps while taking action to close the gap.

becoming
a powerBuilder

Challenge...

I find myself below 0 on the Leadership Score.

Potential Steps...

When we find ourselves disempowered in the emotional states below 0, those who give help *can appear to be a threat.* Our reactions to support can push others away, further reducing our resources.

Recognize that being in survival or fight-or-flight mode is a symptom of a score below 0.

Practicing gratitude for what we already have can help. We have so much more than we give ourselves credit for having. That is part of how we got into a comparative game that created the fight-or-flight response.

Cultivate enough courage to turn around what feels like a downward spiral. Foster responsibility and empathy to resolve any difficult life circumstances or relationships that reinforce these lower states.

Creating a habit to relax before decision making -- *like baths, silence, massage* – can change a stress state into intelligent mode. *Fear-based decisions can be suspect. Relaxed-state decisions can be less destructive.*

Challenge...

My thoughts are out of control.

Potential Steps...

A great many of our thoughts are like a burp that results from "programming indigestion." It is less of a problem that we *have* thoughts than that we *identify* with them. If I have a thought that says to me, "I am unhappy," I can notice that and simply move on. But most of us don't do that. We take the thought and make it the starting point to our next downward spiral. We make a story around *why* we are not happy. And we continue to share that story with those in our lives.

Listen and assess if the thought is misfiring old recordings or if it is a supportive command, need, idea, or thought. This is a way to practice using the intelligent mode while helping to eliminate the accumulation of new limiting beliefs.

Forego the temptation to identify with your thoughts.
   Don't engage it or tell a story about it.

Practice being in the driver's seat of your human complex.
   Mindfulness practice is about being completely present in the activity we are doing with our entire human complex. This takes practice. Maybe I can spend 3 seconds typing these words while consciously feeling the keys before I go on autopilot mode again. Next time -- 5 seconds. More practice, more benefit!

Challenge...

I want to stop projecting the contents of my bucket on others.

Potential Steps...

The most complete way to stop projecting is to resolve the programming bugs in the bucket. Until then, be very present to what is going on around you and inside of you. If you *think* someone feels a certain way, unconfirmed by them, *you are projecting.* Your assumption may be correct – sometimes -- but your projection came from faulty belief filters and activated traumas in your bucket.

Understand that we ALL project. That is the nature of having a perspective. With work, our projections become less disruptive to our lives and our relationships.

Blaming (or shaming) others is usually a rich place to find where we are projecting.

What did you do to make the situation happen?

Are you staying in a job with a Dominator boss without doing anything about it?

Does someone behave in a way that you don't like, while you do it too and don't like it in yourself? "You lie, drink too much, overeat, interrupt, etc."

We need to do this work on ourselves -- only.

Others are responsible for themselves.

Sometimes this means changing our beliefs or handling a trauma. Sometimes this means changing a relationship or a job. Listen to yourself and do what is right for you.

Challenge...

I find boundaries to be a confusing topic.

Potential Steps...

Boundaries are like rules. When we have a boundary, we can feel it and be clear with others about what we find acceptable or not. Boundaries are complicated by the contents of our buckets. Some of our rules come from faulty programming. We may not want to uphold uninspected rules – or expectations – that we feel in our human complex.

When you feel a negative feeling, notice what was said or done by you or someone else in that moment. *This is intelligent mode.*

How do you feel about what was said or done? Was their behavior appropriate? Determine if your feeling was appropriate.

Example: I feel upset that my boss selected another employee to present our team project. I consciously understand that the person was chosen because they worked twice as many hours on the project as anyone else. Therefore, I know this is a programming "bug" inside of me. I realize that I have a trauma or a belief I need to find that caused this feeling to arise. I work with an EFT & Matrix Reimprinting practitioner. We find a childhood experience when a bully stole my homework and turned it in as his own. I got in trouble with the teacher. I decided that I would always present my own work – no matter what. That's why I felt bad about my colleague!

Challenge...

I want to use what I have learned through life's challenges.

Potential Steps...

Every compensation in life can be recycled into an effective tool in a healthy environment with a healthy bucket. If one has healed from exhibiting Surrenderer traits, they may be more enabled to spot Dominators and to know what healthy boundaries are. Others who haven't been through the same experience may not realize what boundaries are, how they can support, and how unhealthy ones can hinder us. A person in a less safe upbringing might be hyper-vigilant as a compensation. They may be able to use that to spot character traits and flaws, along with the contents of others' buckets, and respond with compassion. Finally, when a healthy bucket is back in place, Dominator traits can help in a stressful situation where calm and collected strategizing and executing is necessary. In this case, it is strategizing instead of manipulating, because this healthier bucket is creating, *not* competing for power.

What do you find easy to do that others find difficult? This could point to areas where you have learned to compensate during challenges.

Example: Develop many possibilities to solve a single problem.

How can those traits be converted and used to support your power to create?

Example: Use possibility thinking in a brainstorming session.

Challenge...

What entry points can increase my Power to Create.

Potential Steps...

Our use of language, attachment to thoughts, unconscious beliefs, bodily sensations, feelings, emotions, and 5 senses can all be entry points to increased power. This can be a complicated, but fun, part of doing this work. Our experience of life is like that of a kaleidoscope.

When one part of the human complex changes, our whole view changes.

Use empowering language patterns to begin to shift all of the unconscious patterns. Something as simple as changing a pattern of constantly say "no" to everything into saying "yes" to supportive events, people, or projects would begin to shift the programming of the entire human complex.

Look at creating similar changes in your relationship to your thoughts and beliefs.
Change "I don't know" to "I'll find out." And do!

Be mindful of your internal and external senses.
Feel the water on your hands when washing dishes.
Notice the feeling that comes up and look at triggers.
Hear yourself when you say, "I can't do that."

Any small changes that are implemented will give us more power to make more changes.

Challenge...

My body doesn't feel like it is supporting me.

Potential Steps...

The body affects our bucket and vice versa. Both can increase or diminish the availability of our Power to Create. Poor-quality food lowers ability. It lowers mood. It lowers responsibility. It lowers capability to see and process the barriers in the bucket, which would release more Power to Create.

Stop eating foods that are low in energy and hard for the body to process.

Study basic nutrition, meal timing, hydration, cleansing practices, structure, exercise, and sleep. Healthy cells are better able to support our ability to see and process the contents of the bucket.

Healthy physical practices and habits are so key to feeling good on all levels of the human complex. Adopt **your** best habits.

How much sleep do you really need? Get it.
What foods make you most energetic and healthy?
What exercise habits work best for you?
How much water do you need to drink?
How do you ensure you get that water?

Be the captain of your own ship.

Well done!!
Now you have an idea of some
of the places where your power
has been leaking out. You should
have some idea of the first steps
you can take to begin to
reprogram, handle, and resolve
the issues that have revealed
themselves so far. Take the
step that is clear to you now.
That can often lead to the
next step to continue resolving
these power-sucking programming
bugs. Let's look now at my
favorite tool to resolve traumas
and poorly programmed beliefs.

conversation with Karl Dawson

This is a conversation between Karl Dawson and myself. We were looking to further illuminate the troubleshooting process to help you find and resolve the "bugs" in your human complex.

Karl is the creator of a highly effective technique that helps to resolve the negative effects of both traumas and limiting beliefs. Karl is one of only 28 Founding Master EFT Practitioners in the world and the creator of the Matrix Reimprinting technique. Karl has helped thousands of clients resolve their traumas, along with the hard-coded limiting beliefs which are created during traumatic moments. Karl is an author and trainer with Hay House Publishing Company, having co-authored two books -- *Matrix Reimprinting* and *Transform Your Beliefs, Transform Your Life*.

I trained with Karl in England last year and subsequently became a practitioner in both EFT and Matrix Reimprinting. Let's take a look at what we can do with our traumas and beliefs to increase our Power to Create.

Kelly: Hi, Karl. Great to connect with you again. And thank you for giving us your time and expertise around traumas and limiting beliefs. Can you tell us a little bit about EFT and Matrix Reimprinting?

Karl: Hi, Kelly. Glad to be here. As for EFT and

Matrix Reimprinting, one of the trainers in America came up with a great analogy of the two. EFT is like a movie and Matrix is like a play. EFT works by tapping on the meridian points.

Kelly: The meridians are the body's energy pathways. These are the pathways acupuncturists and shiatsu practitioners use to clear energy blocks affecting our physical, emotional, mental, or spiritual well-being. With EFT, we are tapping on those same energy pathways.

Karl: That's right. As we tap on specific meridian points, we clear the information in various energy fields in our body. If EFT is done properly, you would identify a client's problem -- which could be an addiction, a personality problem, a phobia, an allergy, or whatever it might be. We have techniques to trace the problem back to a specific memory.

With EFT, the analogy would be like looking at a movie. We watch movies all the time. We might like dramas or scary films or sad films. In EFT, the films we are watching are from our lives -- from our past, our early lives, and our childhoods. When we look at the memory with EFT, we start to re-experience the feelings. This flow of energy comes back into the body as, for example, a sick feeling in the stomach, a tight feeling in the chest, or a blockage in the throat. As we experience these feelings, tapping on these very powerful meridian points clears that information and clears that energy. So, at the end of running through a specific traumatic memory, we have a completely different relationship to it. We don't feel the same way about it. In addition, we also have a change in thoughts. We experience it differently.

Once the memories become conscious, we see it from the perspective of the person who is stuck in that moment. So, we clear the trauma by tapping the meridian points, and we look at that memory afterward. We see that "oh, I was just a child, and I was doing the best that I could." Or we have other cognitive shifts. But with the EFT technique, the memory would stay the same.

However, with Matrix Reimprinting, the experience is more akin to watching a play. When the memory *is* like a play, we can interact within the memory. We are the director of our own plays. These moments of trauma are stuck in time in our subconscious. Doing this work is literally like stepping back in time. We imagine stepping into the memory. A part of our consciousness re-enters the memory at the point in which we were traumatized.

Kelly: When we use EFT to help us bring up the memory, it can almost feel like magic the first few times. The subconscious will bring into the conscious mind a traumatic experience with which we can interact.

Karl: That's right. In Matrix Reimprinting, we bring up the memory and see our younger selves in that memory. Unlike with EFT -- where we tap on ourselves, our physical body -- in Matrix, we would tap directly on this younger self within the memory.

We refer to the younger self as an ECHO (Energetic Consciousness Hologram). These are like energetic holograms of our younger selves. They are actually very real. We would tap on them and free them from that traumatic moment. And that allows them to move forward. Then we just help them to create a better outcome. What we are doing with Matrix is very different. We are changing the direction of the play.

With EFT, we resolve the trauma of a memory. But with Matrix, we resolve the trauma *and* change what we see, remember, and -- most importantly – what we decided from that day, the belief.

Kelly: I equate EFT work to releasing the injury, or freeze, to our nervous system. I call these injuries "emotional bullets." And with EFT, I can tap on the meridian points, so my body can release the injury and allow the energy to flow the way it is intended. This is a very important part of the work. But it doesn't seem to resolve enough of what I refer to as the contents of the "emotional doggy bag." The contents are the overflow in sensory processing during the overwhelm of a traumatic moment. They became a part of this special recording process.

That is why Matrix is critical for handling the contents of the memory, including the beliefs we created. Additionally, we continue to attract similar adverse circumstances that resemble the unresolved trauma memory – the play. But with Matrix, we can help the younger self, the ECHO, to find the resources that resolve the situation. The ECHO couldn't resolve the issue at that time based on feeling isolated, limited, and unsupported. But they can move through the scene and resolve it now – with our help.

EFT releases the freeze in the energy flow of the nervous system while Matrix releases the play – including the decisions or beliefs – and resolves them in an empowering way.

Having covered an overview of EFT and Matrix, I am going to back us up a bit now. What are traumas? And is there a difference between the sort of garden variety, every day trauma versus a bigger trauma?

Karl: We will put physical traumas -- like falling down and breaking a leg -- to one side. We are talking about events that are emotionally traumatizing rather than physical traumas.

We separate emotional traumas into two types. We have big "T" Traumas: a car crash, being mugged, abused, sexually abused, raped, a tsunami or earthquake, the death of somebody close to you. The really big traumas in life.

Whereas small "t" traumas are more about the decisions you make in reaction to an event. So, you could be in school and the teacher says, "Oh, you stupid child. You go to the back of the class." Or your parent says, "Go away! I am busy right now." These can be traumatic for a young child.

To be traumatized, all you need is two key elements:
1. To feel powerless and
2. To have a threat to your safety or well-being.

So, imagine a primary caregiver says to a young child, "Go away! I'm busy." The child needs that primary caregiver in that moment and is just sent away. The child is not listened to or cared for in that moment. This could create a small "t" trauma. With small "t" traumas, we make decisions in that moment: "nobody loves me," "I'm stupid," "what I want doesn't matter," and all of these potentially thousands of different beliefs that we have developed throughout our lives.

Kelly: The small "t" traumas are called attachment

traumas. We are missing the healthy attachment or connection that we need with our caregivers – if only in that one moment. It doesn't seem like a big deal, and everybody has a moment in which they are not present enough for the child's needs. But these can cause a trauma, and children will subsequently create a belief that affects their lives.

Experiencing a number of these small "t" traumas or big "T" traumas can create in the child Dominator or Surrenderer behaviors. The traumas can cause a loss of our real self at a deep level. Sometimes it creates a loss of our connection to our power supply, based on the injury and beliefs that were hard-coded in the nervous system and subconscious mind. These beliefs will sit alongside the hard-coded beliefs that are programmed in our formative years. We need to realize we have these beliefs, created in those vulnerable, traumatic moments.

Karl: Yeah, and another important thing to remember is that these events go deep into the subconscious. Things go to the subconscious in a variety of ways. Learning experiences are a key one. We have learning experiences that will go into the subconscious. But more powerful than that is trauma, which will go -- as you said -- very deep. It is hard-wired because it is life and death.

If we equate it to the animal kingdom – as if we are gazelles in the plains of Africa – we've got one chance to learn that the cheetah is going to kill us. Once we've picked up that lesson, we never forget it for the rest of our lives.

That's the thing with these traumatic memories -- especially in the early years. We are in a constant state of hypnosis before the age of 6. Any significant events go very deep. They become hard-wired. And once they are there, that becomes our pattern. Once we have a belief like "I am stupid," we will spend the rest of our lives looking for proof of it. We will create events that support that belief and attract these events into our lives. We create, we look for proof, and we attract. The belief also dictates how we react. And these reactions keep adding similar kinds of traumas and make them bigger and bigger. We globalize the problem. From there comes the stress and anxiety that leads to all kinds of problems, both physical and mental.

Kelly: So, we need to be concerned about them and resolve them because they seem to pop up on a day-to-day basis for us.

Karl: Absolutely. Some beliefs -- like "I'm unlovable" or "I'm not good enough" -- can be recreated every day of our lives. We start to look for it. We'll look for evidence of it. It's just like if you buy a new red car, you'll see all these red cars everywhere. It's your subconscious making all of these connections. And that's what happens with beliefs as well.

So, our early childhood experiences set the blueprint for the rest of our lives. It's hard-wired, but it's the subconscious. And that's the key. That's where the problem lies with these early memories. There is so much clinical evidence in every area of medicine that points to so many illnesses being related to stress. And the distress goes back to childhood events.

It all comes down to the beliefs we make during these moments of our lives in which we are traumatized. We make decisions because we have to. In that moment, we make a decision that the picture in our subconscious means "I am stupid" or "I am unlovable" or "people will reject me" or whatever it is.

The pictures and the meanings are the language of our subconscious.

Kelly: I have spent the last 3 years trying to find the best tools available to resolve the issues with the human complex – the entirety of me.

I wanted to know what would handle my traumas on a belief level, on a tissue level, and in the brain. In essence, how can I rewire the brain, reprogram the nervous system, and adjust the contents of the subconscious mind? I found many resources: Daniel Amen's SPECT brain scans – complete with an extensive plan, various types of specialized talk therapy, EMDR therapy (Eye Movement Desensitization and Reprocessing), neurofeedback, somatic work on the body, and a list of 100s of more therapies, practices, and tools. I have looked at numerous experts in this area – including Peter Levine and Bessel van der Kolk – who happens to be right here in the Boston area where I am.

I don't consider any single tool to be a one-size-fits-all. I love that we have several ways to address the issues that we deal with in our human complexes. I think many tools can chip away at certain parts of the traumas that each of us carry.

I have found EFT with Matrix to be my most effective tools. There is something about EFT and Matrix that releases the trauma from my nervous system, but also enables me to go into the story to examine the belief. I have been able to go back to my mother and ask her about situations that occurred when I was one-year-old and two-years-old

-- which I shouldn't consciously remember -- and the details are accurate to her recollection.

What is your opinion of EFT and Matrix along with other therapies, when it comes to traumas and beliefs?

Karl: Anybody who trains with me will know that I am a big advocate of having many tools. Some of them I recommend more than others. Obviously to me, it's all about EFT and Matrix. But I do realize there are many other therapies – NLP, hypnotherapy, and talk therapy has its place, obviously. But to really make an effective change, you have to get to the subconscious, and you have to change the pictures.

There are certain therapies that will very quickly change beliefs. That doesn't make sense to me because you've still got these pictures and the meaning of these pictures. You're still going to keep reacting to them over and over. Nothing changes subconsciously.

As long as the therapy is looking at the subconscious, that is the key element. And the power of Matrix is that we are going back to the moment when we made these decisions. It's like we have little parallel lives stuck in these moments throughout our subconscious. And they really are determining the whole direction of our lives – these moments and these decisions. We can go back there, and we can realize it. Literally, it's like stepping back in time. Energetically, we are there, and we can communicate with these ECHOs, these younger versions of ourselves.

We can only consciously process a tiny bit of information. But the subconscious is processing 40 million bits of information per second. By going back there, we can understand all of the thoughts, the feelings, the emotions, and what actually happened – not just a section of what happened. Within a trauma, we go into the stress response – in this case we freeze -- and we turn off the higher processing part of the brain. We look for anything that seems dangerous, like mixed signals, expressions, and body posture. As you said, going back there is very real. You have spoken to your mother, and she confirmed what you saw in the memory. These moments are locked in that space and time -- stuck in that moment. That's what Matrix allows you to do, which I don't think many therapies do.

EFT is wonderful for the resolution of trauma and is obviously a big part of Matrix. This brings us to the somatic work that you also mentioned. I began to realize that releasing the trauma of a memory makes a difference -- especially for a big "T" trauma. But when it's the small "t" traumas, it's more about the beliefs that were decided in that moment. Matrix allows us to understand exactly what we made the event mean. I find it fascinating that there are thousands of people I've worked with who are blown away when we go in there. They realize "*That* was the decision that I made that day." Then they think "Oh my God! My whole life -- I can see that decision everywhere!" They have gotten to 50, 60, 70-years-old, and their whole lives have been run by these decisions they were completely, blissfully unaware of. The impact and power of these beliefs affect the work we do, how we conduct our day-to-day life, and how we react to situations. I think that's the power of Matrix. It is seeing what these decisions are *and* seeing the effect that they have had on our lives -- and being able to change them.

Kelly: I often find that the work I do on myself

is getting much easier than when I started this process. Depending on how much of this work and what type of work I am doing, sometimes it can still be challenging. To make this real, what should somebody expect in their lives – both positive and challenging – if they decide to do this trauma and belief work?

Karl: If you don't do some work, your life is just going to get worse and worse. I'm sure anybody working on being a more powerful leader will see that. He thinks "I'm getting older and wiser, but why are the problems getting worse? Why does this anxiety just get worse? Why is the infection getting worse? Why is my addiction getting worse?" Basically, this globalization occurs – we just keep adding and adding to the traumas and beliefs. So, ultimately, if we don't do something about this stuff, the body will tell us to do something about it. A lot of times, we get sick. And on the other side of the sickness or on the other side of the "dark night of the soul" – when our whole life collapses -- we realize that was our subconscious telling us we have to change.

We can't get away without doing the work. It's a necessity -- sooner or later.

Unfortunately, in our current system, so many people end up on drugs, with all of the operations and all of the health problems. And these could be averted by simply dealing with these negative beliefs and traumas.

It can feel like a downside in the early days of doing this work, depending on what beliefs you managed to create in childhood that have affected you. Gary Craig, the creator of EFT, used to have this metaphor: "We live in a forest of trees, and each of those trees is like a specific memory. It's an issue. You are just constantly bumping into these trees. Everywhere you turn, you're bumping into a tree." So, in the early days, when you start this work, you're going to bump into some trees. It *can* be painful to start to understand and to revisit these memories and see how they affected your life. But pretty soon, life starts getting better. There are fewer trees. You find you're sleeping better, you're less anxious, less depressed. You don't feel the need for the addictive materials anymore -- drugs or drink or food or whatever it is. Life just gets better and better. The pains go. You have more time and happiness and joy instead of misery and worry and anxiety.

It *is* a process. And it depends on what you're working on. If it's just a simple phobia, you might be in a session with a practitioner for 30 minutes. The phobia of 30 years – of dogs or snakes or spiders – is gone. But if it's one of these deep-seated beliefs, you could be working away for months or years. But life will change. When you go directly to the beliefs, you realize: "My hearing is better. My sight is better. Or I'm losing weight." A lot of things start to change when you work directly with beliefs. It is a case of doing some work, then going back out into the world with the thought: "Oh things have adjusted. I'm attracting differently now. I'm creating differently. I'm reacting differently to situations." Then, you do a bit more work, and you just notice that your life starts to get better instead of worse.

Kelly: Since *Creating a Leader* is about increasing our power to create, I would love to know who you are today as a result of resolving many of your traumas and limiting beliefs.

Karl: I came to understand that my issue is always about feeling second best to the most powerful person around me. It would be the top person in the classroom or the leader in a gang. When I married, I chose a very powerful woman. So, I was always put down and kept in my place. That has been one of my big beliefs and my big pattern. I have recreated this in the workplace, home, everywhere – my whole life. And it doesn't sound like the worst thing, but it is when that person is so powerful you're not allowed to excel at anything. In childhood, you aren't even able to talk. They'll talk over you or they'll just say "shut up."

Because of this, I strove to feel better, to feel a bit more powerful within myself. I wanted to feel powerful in my own right -- not Robin to Batman or Tonto to the Lone Ranger. Through this work, I began to understand that this was my driving force throughout the years.

When I became a practitioner, I had come from a very, very bad place. I went through a divorce. I had a lot of incredible pain all over my body. I had a collapsed disc in my lower back. I had neck pain, shoulder pain, and knee pain. I had all signs of a lack of self-worth.

To start to find my power, I took on a new role, being a practitioner. I got comfortable there. So, then I moved to the next level to become a trainer. Then I worked really hard to be the best I could as a trainer. Then I came to a point where I realized I was as good as the other trainers. Then I went to the next level – I was one of only about 28 EFT Founding Masters in the world. It was a very small group, so the group got a lot of limelight. I was completely out of my depth. As the year went on, I developed further and further and began to feel equal to them. Next, I wrote this book on Matrix Reimprinting in 2009. The book was picked up by Hay House Publishing Company, which is the leader in our area – the self-help world. And now I'm suddenly in the middle of some of the biggest names in the world – Wayne Dyer, Bruce Lipton, and Louise Hay herself. And I'm presenting on stage. So, I'm being listened to – which used to be a big issue – about *being listened to.*

The day I presented at a Hay House conference, I had Gregg Braden following my talk. I was in the green room with Caroline Myss. The issue I had has made me always strive -- to be better and to move on to the next level every time. With the work that I have done, with EFT and Matrix, I've allowed that to happen.

Realizing what the issue is -- what the belief is -- is so important. It gives you direction on what you're doing. You're not just doing it subconsciously. You have the awareness of what you're trying to achieve. That's important.

Kelly: What are the steps somebody could take to get started on this type of work for themselves?

Karl: You can read more about traumas, beliefs, EFT, and Matrix Reimprinting in a book that I co-authored with Kate Marillat called *Transform Your Beliefs, Transform Your Life.*

The simplest way to get started is through the EFT and Matrix practitioners throughout the world.

There is the www.matrixreimprinting.com website.

Every city in America and every country in the world will likely have EFT practitioners. And this work can be done at a distance, by telephone or Skype.

To work with the *beliefs*, I'd certainly recommend working with a Matrix practitioner. The next step up from that would be to take a course. We train a wide variety of professions including doctors, psychiatrists, psychologists, hypnotherapists, massage therapists, and energy practitioners. We train individuals who are ill and want to get better, but their medical path is not helping them. There are others who are just interested in this area, and they'll take the course as well. Whatever background you're coming from, just take the course for your own reasons. We have trainers in many countries and trainers who are willing to travel as well.

Find a practitioner. Experience it. See how powerful it is. And then look at learning more about it -- even if you don't want to become a practitioner. Just learn for your own advancement, realization, and understanding of what your world is about.

Kelly: Thank you so much, Karl, for sharing your expertise and personal experiences with us. I can only imagine it will give the reader a greater understanding, along with steps to directly improve their power to create as leaders.

Karl: Wonderful! Thank you so much, Kelly.

In this Troubleshooting chapter, we have looked at several individual challenges and the steps to begin to resolve them. Then Karl Dawson brought us through EFT and Matrix Reimprinting. He shared the benefits they both have in removing the freeze from the nervous system, re-recording the video that was playing below our conscious awareness, and adjusting the decision that was made during the overwhelming experience. *Keeping It Real* is the final section in this in-depth chapter. I wanted to share some perspective in an attempt to keep the work from feeling too overwhelming.
I hope it helps.

keeping it real

On the day I was born, my mother almost died giving birth to me. She even had a near-death experience. That wasn't my *fault*, and it certainly wasn't her *fault*. I didn't get to meet and be with her in the first critical days after being born, and that has had an impact on my entire life. My mother told me this when I was 25. But it wasn't until I was 47 that I started to see what happens to our programming when we are not given what we need at critical points in life.

I share this small part of my story because I want to emphasize just how much *nobody is at fault* for what happens with our programming. A fault-finding focus steals our attention and is a form of competing. It won't help us to improve our ability to create – which is the whole point of this work.

For 45 years, I didn't understand why my human complex wouldn't go in the direction that I would intend it to go. Weary of experiencing such frustration, I turned over every stone looking for ways to fulfill my ability to create meaningfully and purposefully. I realized that I was undertaking a tremendous adventure.

I do identify myself as an adventurer. I have accomplished things just because I thought it would be fun to do them, without regard for the difficulty involved.

Some examples include making an album of 9 songs of my own music with the help of a few friends. I also ran the New York Marathon. I have inline skated 100 miles in a day and kayaked 31 miles in a day. I am self-taught to do both video work and animated video work. I have turned around companies that were almost out of business. I trained companies all over the US and Europe, while running two European organizations. I traveled around the world with Anthony Robbins as a trainer and an executive coach. I have studied with leaders in their fields all over the world. I am almost finished writing a 3-book series. And I have visited and explored all seven continents.

Yet, the work found in this book series is different. It is like climbing the Mt. Everest within each of us. It is the inner adventure that most of us are unaware exists, ready to be explored.

Like a real trek up Mt. Everest, a base camp is critical to the success of this adventure. The base camp consists of the support factors necessary to success. Some of those for me are the right teachers, professionals in various fields, research, and a tremendously clear vision of myself creating at a +10-level of fulfillment.

I frequently find my +10 flow mode now. It is not consistent if I go too far beyond my current comfort zone during the process of creating. An example of this was the endeavor to write 3 books. To support the readers of my books, I have taken speaker training at both the National Speakers Association and Toastmasters. During a different training from these two organizations, geared toward speakers and writers, I unconsciously adopted a higher standard (rule about quality) for my books and presentations than I was capable of producing. That caused a great deal of anxiety for me, ending a 3-4 month run of daily flow mode.

That process revealed the need to adjust my standard, while rapidly improving my skills. And I needed to work on internally generating and acknowledging my value and worth for myself. This was a great opportunity to recognize a place where I was adopting others' viewpoints to tell me how good or bad I was or my books were.

As part of working through the missing steps to valuing my own worthiness -- while ensuring it wasn't dependent on my accomplishments -- I looked for resources that could help me move back into flow mode.

First, I needed to understand that nothing would change inside of me if I was looking outside to blame others for where I found myself today. That approach is a trap that keeps us stuck. In that place, we lack compassion for others and struggle to maintain healthy boundaries – whether too strong or too weak.

I needed to understand what this animal called self-esteem was, if I was to improve it and stabilize flow mode. I found many teachers in this area, all of whom contributed to my progress. One teacher, Darlene Lancer, provided her model of levels of self-esteem. This would coordinate with the work that I was doing around the Leadership Score. I adjusted some language and content and constructed the *Self-Worth Scale*.

This scale helps us to see that anytime we are generating value and self-worth from an external source, this devalues and destabilizes our ability to be in intelligent mode. We are stuck in autopilot mode and waiting for others to tell us how good we are. We are crushed when they don't tell us that. The challenge is that they can never tell us something that will satisfy our need to value ourselves. We are the only source of that value, if it is to be lasting and not fleeting.

We must find our personal approval seeker that was trained to look to the outside for self-worth and feeling valued. We need to teach this seeker to look inside, not out-side to accomplishments, relationships, or circumstances. Each of us is a highly valuable individual without ever doing a single thing. Until we can learn this lesson, we are wired for pain and unfulfilled potential. We will always seek others scraps of approval for what we are *doing*.

the self-worth scale

power to CREATE		SELF-WORTH
+10	creating	self-love
		self-compassion
		self-acceptance
0	neutral	self-esteem (valuing self from within)
		below 0 -- worth generated by other people or through accomplishments
-10	competing	**FAKE BUCKET** (unable to value self)

There are so many ways that a person could be programmed to look outside for approval. It could come from a parent who wasn't present enough to supply the care and develop-ment that the child needed. The child associated that, uncon-sciously, with not being worthy of getting his needs met. He would try to deny how he really felt to accommodate and appease the caregiver. For example, a father only leaves work to watch the games if his son is pitching in the championship each year. The child recognizes and creates a belief that...

...he is only valuable if he wins.

The daughter only gets attention from her mother if she is willing to help her prepare dinner. The little girl doesn't make friends after school because she needs this attention from her mother. She decides that *she isn't worthy of attention unless she is helping* and *she isn't allowed to have friends*. This could be the beginning point of the loss of self-worth and value, feeling like ourselves, and clarity of our own needs.

If you add television to the mix -- exacerbated by a society dependent on advertisements -- you can see why folks can tend to "get in line" with the thoughts, actions, and behaviors that are acceptable. This becomes mass stuck autopilot mode and the opposite of leadership.

To get to a point where we are generating our own approval for ourselves, it is important to go inside. But what the hell does that *really* mean? What is this internal Mt. Everest crap that seems to only exist to a few people? Well, those were my thoughts as I went through the process. Turns out, they were onto something profound and important.

I learned that if I stop and really look at how I am *internally experiencing* a person or situation, I can behave in full support of my own needs. If I don't look at how I *feel inside*, I continue a life-long habit: either going with someone else's clarity and best interest, at worst, or my programmed response, at best. That moment of pause and quality internal reflection is the difference between -10 and +10 leadership. It is a simple pause that reveals our internal experience to us. That experience is honored by us when we respond respectfully to the other person, either with a boundary or unabashedly sharing our own opinions and viewpoints. We become less concerned about their responses, as that no longer determines our value or worth. Meanwhile, we continue to create improved circumstances in life to ensure that only those who will mind our boundaries and treat us well are welcome to play with us. All of this is *simple*, but not necessarily *easy*.

Imagine the dashboard of a car. If I notice that I "red line" my car while driving fast, I wouldn't press the gas down further. I would potentially hurt the car. The same occurs with our internal dashboard, based on feelings – instinctive (biological programming) *and* intuitive (gut) – that guide our operations. Learning to drive includes learning the dash board for our human experience. And learning how to stop overriding the information that is provided.

Once I know how I feel about an experience – including my fears of survival and all the other stuff that may come with it -- I can begin some serious self-care. I can take care of my concerns as attentively as I would for a child for whom I am responsible. Sometimes that includes getting the need handled -- like changing a job. Sometimes that means addressing the concern so that it isn't sitting there from an earlier time in my life – like handling a retriggered trauma. This is a pathway to the higher levels of self-worth. In the process of becoming clear around this, my mind started a new tantrum. What *is* this self-care crap? Can that really help me to be a better leader, producing at higher levels of quantity and quality? In a word, YES!

For many of us who want to "charge the hill," so to speak, this work becomes far more difficult. We have learned to keep going – without regard to the cost to ourselves. *Healthy surrender* for this group, of which I feel I am a part, can be experienced as more like giving up. For those of us who have fought through our entire lives, this seems like an impossible task to ask of ourselves. I assure you – it is not giving up, and it is not impossible. Keep "charging the hill" and the likely outcome over time is an erosion of power to create. Going to the internal mountain climbing experience fosters surprising improvements in your life.

When we ignore our gut when it expresses fears or other emotions, we lose the opportunity to release and integrate the invisible chains that bind us. I recognized that the younger versions of me spoke out to make me pause before I went forward. With some check ins, some trauma handlings, and adjusted limiting beliefs, I now can see more clearly what *I* really want to do. I act on that. In some cases, listening to my entire human complex creates only a very slight change to my approach. But the internal experience becomes completely different. Over time, the fight-or-flight responses in my complex occur less often. This results from the self-care that helps us to increase our self-worth.

I also recognized that when I didn't acknowledge what was happening inside and care for myself at a very high level, others wouldn't treat me well either. It was only when I was treating myself extremely well that others would do the same. If they happened to treat me poorly, I would tell them that it wasn't okay to do that. If that didn't take care of it, I would remove them from creating a negative impact on my self-worth and my life.

The "Secret" Handshake

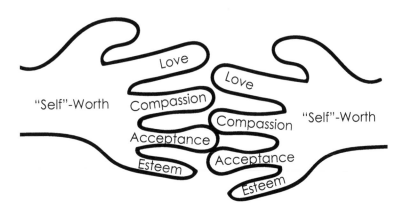

Thus, I don't concern myself with Dominators or Surrenderers as much now. Imagine if you were to hold your hand in front of you with your fingers stretched out completely, as if you were going to shake hands with your fingers opened wide. Each of your fingers represents the different levels of self-worth. An outstretched hand points your self-esteem outward from yourself, while asking (or begging) others to give you your self-worth. That is NOT *self*-worth. Others *can't* give *self*-worth to us.

A person with fingers outstretched (Surrenderer) is looking for a match who also has outstretched fingers -- like two puzzle pieces. They are doing this because this is how they were programmed early on to *get* self-worth for themselves.

Of course, we know that any person asking for self-worth is already in a losing game. When another person comes along (Dominator) and shows the self-worth seeker that her fingers fit right into his, he is now thrilled that he has "self-worth" *from* her. She is also thrilled that he is willing to give his power *and* her self-worth *to* her. She is unable to give herself value and worth and is cut off from her own creative power source.

To handle this for both, each of them can do the equivalent of closing the hand into a fist. The fingers now point inward to each of these individuals. That means each level of self-worth is brought into the possessors' responsibility to provide it for himself or herself. When we provide ourselves with our own worth and care and esteem and acceptance and compassion and love, we are more whole and interdependent.

Let's look at these two fists when they get together. You have two whole people who love themselves and are not trying get the other person to complete them. And the knuckles of the fists fit beautifully together. Two whole people who are not trying to unconsciously get their needs met by making the other person behave in any way are now relating in life through healthy interdependence. Everyone in this condition is better off for having known one another.

A fist doesn't mean closed to others. It means when we do interact, we don't lose ourselves in the process. We also don't require others to build a "self" for us. That is exhausting to do for ourselves, much less for someone else. We simply "fist bump" through a fulfilling connection and experience the world in a very healthy way. We don't express a loss of ourselves through an illogical interlocking type of handshake that will ultimately help no one and probably hurt many in the process.

There is no room for a Dominator or Surrenderer in this fist-bump environment. Even if we just look at the analogy of the hands, the person with outstretched fingers wouldn't have a place to interlock with a person who has a fist (self-love). Neither will be satisfied and both will go their own way. Remember, the one with self-worth is not asking for the other person to complete them. And the one without self-esteem isn't going to feel complete with a self-loving (whole) person who has no internal need to complete, "fix," or take power from someone else.

Closing our fist, so to speak, makes it very clear when others wish us well or not. Taking back our inner knowing, by learning how we feel and honoring that with self-care, helps us to reprogram the approval seeker to stop looking outside at other people or at our accomplishments for self-worth. We become great at loving and caring for the totality of ourselves. What an accomplishment.

Wouldn't it be great to let yourself know how okay it was to have done *everything that you have ever done*? Wouldn't it be great to see yourself in the mirror with softer eyes that share the kind of love a child deserves? Wouldn't it be great to allow yourself to learn what you may not have been taught growing up? These are not only great in theory. They are essential to fulfill your potential as a leader.

From this place, others don't "get to you" or erode your self-worth as easily with their comments or actions. You also get to value others more, as it is no longer a threat to your self-worth to do so. You recognize that as you value others more, they may become uncomfortable with you valuing them much more than they value themselves.

Understanding this internal dynamic (yes, Dominators are there because of what is going on *inside of us*) can help us move to 0 and above on the Leadership Score. 0 is the courageous, responsible starting point in which the act of creating what we can in the world also improves our human complex – all the way up to fulfilling our potential at +10.

Many of us have been taught to appear that we have nothing "wrong" with ourselves. We run from any diagnosis, label, or perceived weakness. Yet, if we embrace areas that are weak or holding us back, we can move through them, and we can find our own gold in life. I have nothing to lose if I consider that I am exhibiting unsupportive behaviors, and then I work on them. When we don't want to look at these impediments, we are usually the only ones who won't see them. They are more obvious to those who are around us. So, we are just playing an unhealthy game with ourselves. It isn't a matter of getting a diagnosis or becoming a hypochondriac, for that matter. It is a healthy and courageous opportunity to assess what is really happening for us, internally and externally, and addressing what comes up. Honesty replaces denial. Anything short of that is like painting our Leadership Score to a higher level and acting like we have attained that level. If we are competing with others and secretly trying to hold them back, we are NOT at +10. That isn't judgement. It is honest and it provides us with a starting point. This work is relatively very fast if we are honest and clear about what is really going on. This work is impossible if we are not willing to look.

In society, weakness has become stigmatized. Anything short of having a perfect front can make us feel bad. This is bullshit, and hopefully you can see that.

The more we look outside for our worth, the more we lose it inside -- which is the only place it can exist.

Learn to listen to yourself. Learn to take care of yourself based on what your entire human complex is telling you. Set your vision for yourself. Creating what YOU want is an internally generated practice. Find what isn't working for *you*, on *your* terms and for *yourself*. Find ways to heal that and upgrade your human complex. And please, care for yourself deeply by being gentle with yourself in the process. Set up the game to win within yourself, for *your* own reasons.

Maybe it's time we run our own race.

Very well done!
That chapter is a bear.
It really does reflect the
experience of troubleshooting
in life -- challenging but doable.
Having the tenacity to get to
get to this point will be very
helpful for you on your
journey to increase your power.
You have completed
the first chapter about the need
for an owner's manual, the
second chapter on operating
instructions, and the third
chapter -- troubleshooting.
Next is a fun chapter about
arriving at higher states of
operating our human complex.
Enjoy this introduction...
you earned it!

CHAPTER FOUR

high-performance
human complex

ascending the leadership score

When we are ready to find flow mode, some of the hardest work is already done...or at least well underway!

We begin to understand our human complex and gain control over it by resolving the bumps and dings. From there, it seems magical that everybody else "suddenly behaves differently," making it easier for us to succeed. In other words, we realize that it was necessary to upgrade our human complex to have enough courage and responsibility to sit comfortably in the driver's seat. This helps us to remove the identity of "victim" of the actions of other human complexes. We are rewarded with an increase in our power to create.

We achieve greater peace that signifies our skillful use of intelligent and autopilot modes to the benefit of those around us. We *develop* ourselves continuously, as a **Leader** who possesses a greater **Power to Create**. With established *visions* being *executed* in an *empowering* manner, we have found our path to the +10-version of ourselves.

It becomes an honor to operate *this* human complex.

We meet this honor with gratitude, compassion, and purposeful service to others.

flow mode

When we are operating our human complex, and have trained it extensively to do specific activities, we may find a paradoxical state that feels both *completely conscious* and *completely consumed* at the same time. The activity that we are doing in that moment feels "bigger than ourselves." From that place, something sacred within us opens, introducing us to the deepest parts of who we are.

> The dancer and the dance are one.
> One cannot exist without the other.
> When we observe "them" merging
> to the most sacred depths of unity,
> a portal opens, inviting each of us
> to find that sacred place within ourselves.

Flow mode is a state that most of us have glimpsed. When we find it, time stands still or leaps into the future. We know that we are a part of something bigger or greater. And it is healing for ourselves and those in our environment.

Flow mode can remain elusive when unresolved issues exist in our autopilot and intelligent modes. Flow mode is more predictable when we restore the other modes, educate ourselves to mastery level, and surrender completely to even the most mundane activity done with great purpose.

This is a state of concurrent total control and no control. This paradox challenges many who seek flow mode. It doesn't exist when we engage in our craft to overcome "inadequacies" created through comparisons. In flow moments, it is *only* about what is created through us right here and right now.

Executives acknowledge flow mode as a secret to their greatest successes. Basketball players cultivate the ability to soar through the air. Artists attract this creative power to sculpt masterpieces. Surfers "become" waves that would have swallowed them alive. Scientists, transformed by this genius, express equations that redefine humanity. Spiritual seekers transcend the limits of human nature through this sacredness.

being "that" good

The path to flow requires practice until autopilot mode is fully programmed to carry out the steps of an activity, without our intelligent intervention. When we are unconsciously controlling the process, genius *can* emerge as an artist, leader, or creator.

To court flow, we create a challenge that is engaging enough for us to stay *fully focused*, while easy enough to help us *remain unconscious to the steps* of the process.

The basketball player has practiced thousands of hours of shooting the ball with opponents in front of him. Because he doesn't need to focus on the mechanics of shooting, he can dance with his opponent until he sees a new way to *create* the magical 3-pointer that seemed impossible.

To cultivate the *unconscious competence* that is supportive of flow, we can self-assess to determine where we might be missing education, training, experience, or supportive beliefs to be *"that" good.*

As we set the appropriate challenge level, fully engage in the activity, and struggle to a point of release, we can eliminate the elusiveness of flow.

This is common practice in extreme sports, as the athletes' lives depend on flow mode for their safe and creative participation.

flow "hacking" through attention

If *the challenge of the dance* is used to create flow for the dancer, then is it possible for the dancer to create flow by *actively pouring herself into the dance*? If we don't have to be so thoroughly entertained from outside to find flow, could we *cultivate flow from within through the skillful use of our attention*?

If we take a page out of Zen wisdom, we can "hack" flow by creating an all-consuming focus for the activity at hand. This eliminates the need to be drawn in by the challenge, turning mundane tasks into potential "flow bait."

Daily tasks, such as washing dishes, can be practiced in a way that we remain completely present with the task itself. We can focus on experiencing the task through our five senses -- fully investing our attention into the *feel* of the warm water and dish, the *sight* of the bubbles and running water, the *smell* of the dinner that lingers, and so on.

When we *adjust any beliefs that limit* our ability to access flow through the *skillful use of attention*, each present moment becomes a portal to flow mode. When we combine a healthy human complex with the skillful use of attention, and mastery of our craft, flow becomes far more accessible.

on becoming a +10 leader...

With skillful use of attention and increased control of our human complex, we will notice certain phenomena on the path to becoming a +10 Leader in flow mode.

Often the most challenging stage of finding flow is the surrender phase. A leader can "power through" from -10 to +9 leadership with very active direction and participation. However, the leap from +9 to +10 is one of, shall we say, *faith*.

The Creative Genius Within

Our first action for cultivating our +10 leadership turns out to be participatory inaction. We remain a witness to the emergence of the creative genius -- although it lays dormant within most of us. This is our internal well-spring of creativity, ideas, and inspiration. It is unique to each of us.

Power Flows through Attention

Because creative genius is unique to each of us, any form of competition -- such as comparisons -- takes our attention and power away from our unique flavor of creating. Attention is the conduit of our creative flow. The masterful use of our attention upon our creation helps us to master flow.

The amount of power inherent in the creativity flowing through the attention channel is based on our general emotional state. Our power in a state of shame, fear, or anger will provide a negative ability to create. When we pass the 0 mark on the Leadership Score, we do it with the aid of emotions and feelings like courage, responsibility, joy, and peace.

Clear, Solid Visions WITH Flexibility

As we surrender enough to watch the emergence of our creative inspiration, we will want to harness this powerful source within to positively impact our environment.

Visions are a very effective tool to direct our attention, to solidify an idea to be created, and to help us use our resources to fulfill our aspirations. Sometimes a seemingly solid vision needs to be adjusted. Flow helps us to have the *flexibility* that is necessary to navigate the best path for fulfillment of *our own* potential.

Tirelessly and Purposefully "Showing Up"

With a clear vision, we "show up" and find the most important priority to materialize our ambitions. We pour ourselves into that task with purpose, *actively encompassed by this moment's activity*. Focusing on being fully engaged in this very moment with this very challenge fosters flow and fulfillment. Then, we move effortlessly to the next challenge. In time, waking up and moving through the day becomes a source of *flowing* from one fulfilling activity to the next. The "work days" of those in flow can tend to get longer. This is a byproduct of the increased energy found from within and through the fulfillment of purpose-driven creations. We stay balanced in life, but we stop getting tired so easily.

Empowering Those We Affect

When we find flow, and are living so purposefully, the byproduct is to make decisions that are positively impacting all who are affected. We can live in a mild to moderate flow state often. In that state, our needs feel like they are constantly being met, leaving no reason to meet our needs at the expense of anyone else. Additionally, the state provides increased access to creativity, making us more skillful and resourceful in deciding the contents of our visions and the best steps to their attainment. Flow stays with us *only* if we are operating in this level of harmony. Empowerment is a path to and a byproduct of flow.

When our intelligence masters the conscious and unconscious elements of our human complex, we can experience the emergence of something that is "greater than ourselves." From that viewpoint, we see our role as being the *steward* of the emerging genius that is "our" creation. *"Arriving" here is akin to finding our home.*

a +10 society

Having a +10 society can be a beautiful dream. The earth's natural processes would be restored, and beauty could abound everywhere. Each of us would feel supported -- collectively and individually -- while realizing new visions that help us to live more naturally and sustainably through flow. We would want to work in this society where we would experience the amazing feelings of creative fulfillment. We would be in harmonious interaction with one another. We would all be steeped in a healthy environment -- one that is inspiring to all, including those who find themselves below +10.
Where could this collective of human complexes go from there?

We are all just little specs on a planet that is rotating at mind-boggling speeds. Each of us is learning how to run our own human complex – on the verge of operating it more in accordance, perhaps, with its maker's specifications.

We can *adjust our limiting beliefs* and *eradicate traumas* and their effects on society that create negative Leadership Scores. Then, I might have to increase the scale on The Leadership Score framework as we find out where flow-life takes us. That would be fine with me!

I'll see you in Creating a Leader: Simply YOU, Stage 3 -- the final book in this series. We will look at the processes of what **Limitless**, **Powerful Leaders** do. We will explore how to *envision* skillfully, *execute* resourcefully, *empower* those involved, and continuously *develop* ourselves.

Remember, we are ALL in this together.

See ya soon . . .

Made in the USA
Middletown, DE
16 June 2017